ORCHID GROWING Illustrated

BRIAN & WILMA RITTERSHAUSEN

Photography by
Andrew Cooper

BLANDFORD PRESS
LONDON · NEW YORK · SYDNEY

First published in the UK 1985
by Blandford Press, Artillery House,
Artillery Row, London SW1P 1RT

Reprinted 1986
Reprinted 1988

Distributed in the United States by
Sterling Publishing Co., Inc.,
2 Park Avenue, New York, N.Y.10016

Distributed in Australia by
Capricorn Link (Australia) Pty Ltd
PO Box 665, Lane Cove
NSW 2066, Australia

British Library Cataloguing in Publication Data

Rittershausen, Brian
  Orchid growing illustrated.
  1. Orchid culture
  I. Title II. Rittershausen, Wilma
  635.9'3415   SB409

ISBN 0 7137 1365 8

*The frontispiece shows part of the Gold
Medal exhibit staged by Burnham Nurseries Ltd
at a recent Chelsea Flower Show of the Royal
Horticultural Society.*

Designed by John Douet

Typeset by August Filmsetting, Haydock, St. Helens
Printed and bound in Portugal by Printer Portuguesa.

CONTENTS

ACKNOWLEDGEMENTS

We would like to express our most grateful thanks to the following firms who kindly assisted us with material for this book.

To Autogrow Products for the pictures on page 42; to Bayliss Autovents Ltd. for the picture on page 47; to C.H. Whitehouse Ltd., for the pictures on pages 40, 41, 44 and 46 (left). To Keith Andrew Orchids Ltd. for allowing us to use their laboratory to produce the pictures on pages 12 and 98 to 102. To Eric Crichton Photos and Priory Orchid Cases for the picture on page 32. To Orchid Sundries Ltd. for their use of equipment used in the pictures on pages 34 to 36. To Burnham Nurseries Ltd. for supplying all plant material, and to Eric Crichton and The Orchid Review Ltd. for the pictures on pages 11, 13 (left) and 14 (left) and the pictures on pages 2 and 112.

Dedicated to our mother

Orchids have been cultivated in the western world for the past 200 years, although they have been known to science for much longer, and were certainly grown by the ancient Chinese.

PART I
THE ORCHIDS

little interest to horticulture. It is the showy species from Asia and South America which have been most easily cultivated and hybridised from and these are certainly the most rewarding to grow.

The arrival of orchids in Europe came about with the age of exploration, and it was the ships' captains who saw a lucrative sideline in bringing back many strange and exciting tropical plants from the new worlds being discovered. Of all the wonders in the plant kingdom it was those early importations of orchids which created the greatest stir and caused sensations. Nothing like the large, flamboyant flowers had ever been seen before. No wonder it became an obsession to grow these beautiful and exotic plants from far-off lands, and no wonder the highest prices were paid, as the wealthy industrialists tried to outbid each other for ownership of the latest arrivals. Since those early times the popularity of orchids has continued to increase as generation after generation of orchid lovers has become completely fascinated by these lovely plants.

It is well known that orchids belong to one of the largest families of plants on earth and that their variety is unsurpassed in the plant kingdom. Their method of growth is a fascinating study in itself: the plants have become so well adapted that they are completely at home in even arctic and temperate regions where they live conventionally in the ground as terrestrials. In warmer tropical and subtropical areas they have developed a completely different method and grow by attaching themselves to trees as epiphytes. Epiphytes are true 'air plants'; they thrive by using the host tree as an anchorage and as a means of getting closer to the light which filters through the forest canopy, but take nothing from the tree for their existence. Instead, they use their long aerial root systems to extract the moisture from the atmosphere which is then stored in their pseudobulbs. Some are known as saprophytes, living on dead or fallen trees, whereas others make their home on rocks and outcrops as lithophytes.

The plants can be found growing at sea level, on the shore line, often subjected to daily salt sprays; others grow very high in mountainous regions, up to 12,000 ft (3,650 m) or more, where snow and frost occur. The orchids are protected from freezing at this altitude by the rarefied atmosphere. There is hardly a place on earth which cannot accommodate some orchid species from marshy swamplands, grasslands and deserts to woodlands and forests. Even subterranean species are known, which live out their whole life cycle completely under the ground, but these are of lesser importance to the horticulturalist.

Although it is true to say that most of the orchid species have been known for almost 100 years, there are areas of the world which are still yielding new species. Every year, new species are being discovered, although these can be small, insignificant plants, which one may well imagine were considered by early plant hunters as of

Originally it was the wild species which were cultivated, but within the last 130 years the raising of man-made hybrids has taken priority. Many of the species are in a sorry state, being almost extinct in the wild, as their habitat is being rapidly destroyed, but at the same time greatly sought after in collections, where they have become rare items indeed. Not all species will readily breed in cultivation and the raising of seedlings is often difficult under artificial conditions. Hybrids often have a wider tolerance of artificial conditions and are a much better proposition for the beginner.

The majority of these hybrids in cultivation have been bred from the epiphytes. These plants retain the unique features of pseudobulbs, leaves and roots, all of which are discussed in the following pages. It will be seen that there is no typical orchid flower or plant. All are vastly different.

Our opening illustration (opposite) shows one of the more extraordinary members of these highly specialised plants. It shows an amazing evolutionary development where the two lateral sepals of the individual flowers which form an umbel have become greatly extended, tapering to fine points. The dorsal sepal, petals and lip are very much smaller and this would be an unassuming flower if it were not for the sepals which extend for over 7 in (18 cm). The cirrhopetalums are related to a much larger genus, the bulbophyllums, and are widely distributed throughout the tropical world.

The genus *Cirrhopetalum* was first described in 1830; there are about 30 species, and not as many hybrids. Elizabeth Anne 'Bucklebury' AM/RHS is one of the most successful hybrids in the genus and was raised by a famous old firm, Stuart Low & Co., in 1969. Its parents are *Cirrhopetalum longissima* and *C. rothschildianum*.

It is a primary hybrid, both parents being species. Primary hybrids are very successful in orchids, and are often the first stage in a very long line of breeding. In the primary hybrid we see the combining of those qualities present in both parent species, and retaining all the charm and natural beauty of the wild flowers. Moreover, being an artificially-produced plant, the resulting hybrids are immediately more vigorous and therefore easier to grow. A further advantage is that those artificially-produced hybrids have grown up in a controlled environment, and unlike the jungle plant it has not had to withstand the rigours of importation and adjusting to unnatural conditions.

The way in which this plant is growing suspended in a pot hanging from the roof is an ideal method of growing epiphytic orchids. The plant has completely encircled the container in which it will remain undisturbed for many years.

FLOWERS

Odontoglossums are one of the most popular genera of orchids in cultivation. They are compact plants – usually requiring only a 4-in (10-cm) pot – with large flowers up to 4 in (10 cm) across, and a dozen or more on a spray. Their somewhat flattened ovoid pseudobulbs are bright green and carry a pair of evergreen leaves from the apex. Several smaller leaves are formed lower down near the base of the pseudobulb. Also from this base from inside one of these lower leaves, comes the flower spike. They have varying flowering seasons, and the flower spike is produced upon completion of the season's pseudobulb. Usually no more than one or two spikes can be expected in a season. The flowers have sepals and petals of equal size, the lip nicely balanced with colourings different from the rest of the flower.

Many of the species are rare, most of the plants in cultivation are hybrids which have greatly increased the colour range, and many of them are intergeneric hybrids. (See *Wilsonara* Tigertalk 'Beacon', page 13.) Mostly the colours are overlaid with bright spotting and flushing, which makes the odontoglossums the most decorative of all orchids. The species occur from Peru through Colombia and Guatemala to Mexico growing as epiphytes mainly at high elevations of between 4,000 and 6,000 feet (1,200–1,800 m). At these altitudes the air is cool and fresh, and these conditions must be imitated for success in cultivation. They cannot stand overheating, and like a shady and moist atmosphere.

Odontoglossum hybrids are better for the beginner. Firstly, if a plant should be lost it is not irreplaceable, whereas some of the species could be. They are generally showier and brighter, with larger flowers, and possess a useful hybrid vigour. They are no more expensive, and often bloom on very young plants. Beginners can easily purchase young plants in flower to grow on to maturity, when their full flowering capacity is realised.

Although odontoglossums are more suited to cool greenhouse culture, the intergeneric hybrids which have been raised from them make very good house plants, being more tolerant and adaptable.

There are very few pests which bother odontoglossums; greenfly may occur on the young buds and slugs and snails have a liking for flower spikes and buds, in addition to attacking the succulent pseudobulbs.

Among the species are a few which need a rest during the winter months. These include *Odontoglossum grande*, and *citrosmum*. Most species and all hybrids do not rest significantly. The only time they are not actively growing is when flowering, when watering is continued.

Odontoglossum hybrids take approximately ten weeks from the time the flower spike is seen to blooming and the flowers will last for six to eight weeks.

Pictured above is *Odontoglossum harryanum* 'Copper' AM/RHS. Its first flowering in England was recorded in 1886, and it was named after Sir Harry Veitch, a great orchid man of his day. Many *Odontoglossum* species grow at high altitudes in the Andes, and are thus cool-growing although close to the equator. Although difficult to raise from seed in cultivation, it has been done, and this species is safe from extinction for the immediate future. Hybrids from it are much easier to raise, and it has been used extensively for breeding.

Cymbidiums are the most widely grown orchids in cultivation. They are also the largest among the widely cultivated types. Their pseudobulbs are large, up to the size of an orange, short and stout. They are sheathed by the bases of the evergreen leaves, which remain intact after the leaves have been shed. The leaves are long, up to 2 ft (60 cm) and about 1–2 in (2.5–5 cm) wide. The flower spikes are stout and can grow up to 3 or 4 ft (90–120 cm) carrying a dozen or more heavily textured flowers 4 in (10 cm) across. These last in perfection for up to eight weeks. They are produced in the late summer and grow throughout the winter to bloom any time from November to May, with the majority flowering in the spring. A large plant may produce up to six flower spikes.

Cymbidiums produce a robust rooting system of thick white roots, and a mature plant may require a 12-in (30-cm) pot, unless divided.

The miniature cymbidiums are smaller in stature and size of flower and are thus easier to accommodate and handle.

The flowers have sepals and petals of similar shape and size, self-coloured with a contrasting lip which is usually white, dotted on the front lobe to a greater or lesser degree with dark red.

Most of the species, mainly from the Far East, with a few in Malaysia and Australia, are rare, and all are considered collectors' items. The modern hybrids have all arisen from about six or eight of the species, but within these were sufficient colours to give the wonderful range to be found in the hybrids today. The only colour lacking is blue.

Cymbidiums are cool-growing orchids which will not flower if grown too warm, or under too much shade, and they do better under controlled greenhouse culture than as indoor plants. Their size is also a drawback as a house plant. If no greenhouse is available, or if the greenhouse overheats in summer, making it unsuitable, the cymbidiums can be summered out of doors for as long as there is no danger of frost. A semi-shady position should be found for them, off the ground, and close to a wall or fence where they will receive the morning or evening sun, but be shaded at midday. With regular spraying and watering the plants will make a much tougher growth, which will result in better flowering productivity.

Cymbidiums grow throughout the year and should be watered continually to keep the plants evenly moist at all times. Feeding can be greatly reduced or stopped altogether for the winter, when there is insufficient light to enable the plant to convert the feed. Feeding during the winter could be harmful to the roots.

There are a number of pests which are unkind to cymbidiums. Red spider mite is probably the worst of these. Small and difficult to see, it can build up into large colonies before any signs are noticed. Check regularly and take precautionary measures to keep plants clean. Scale insects of various kinds will also attack these orchids. They are easier to see, but difficult to eradicate should they get a hold. Greenfly on buds is always a threat, but these are easy to destroy before any harm is done to soft buds.

Repot when necessary immediately after flowering. Remove the flowers by cutting through the stem about 1 in (2.5 cm) from the base after the last flower has been open for about two weeks. Potting can then be done earlier and the plant will have a better spring start. Remove the spike if repotting is not required; it will lessen the strain on the plant at a time when the new growth is getting started.

Pictured here is *Cymbidium* Mirum 'Velmirage' AM/RHS.

Phalaenopsis are the most popular of the warm-growing orchids. They have thick, broad leaves, often attractively mottled in silver or grey. They are monopodial, without pseudobulbs; their leaves grow from a basal rhizome, and usually number between three and six at any time. Their roots are also attractive, being flattened, silvery grey and extensive. Often these roots grow outside the pot and adhere strongly to the bench. The flower-spikes – two or three a year on a mature plant – come from near the base, immediately above a lower leaf. There is no strict flowering season.

They are mainly pink and white, with yellow less frequently seen. The flowers will last for several weeks, and old flower spikes will produce more flowers if cut back to a 'node' along the stem.

In nature phalaenopsis are epiphytic; in cultivation even the hybrids have strong epiphytic tendencies.

The flowers are flat and thinly textured. The two lateral petals are wide, almost obscuring the smaller sepals behind. The lip is small, often brightly coloured. Flowers can be up to 4 in (10 cm) across.

The species originate from Malaysia, Borneo and the Philippines. Some are still grown, but it is mainly the numerous lovely hybrids which fill collections. Phalaenopsis love the heat, and the warmer it is the better they grow. They also like plenty of shade and so are ideally suited to a warm indoor growing case.

These tropical evergreen plants should be grown all year, keeping the compost just evenly moist.

When repotting any aerial roots are best left well alone: inside the pot they will suffocate and die.

The plant above is *Phalaenopsis* Buffin.

Paphiopedilums are the well-known and distinctive 'slipper orchids', their lip resembling a slipper-shaped pouch. They have a large dorsal sepal which stands erect like a sail. It is usually white, and spotted or striped. The lateral petals and pouch are usually similarly coloured, the petals often spotted. The two lateral sepals appear, usually fused into one and mostly out of sight, behind the pouch. Most produce a single flower. The modern hybrids have one large flower up to 6 in (15 cm) across. Some groups of species are two, three or multi-flowered on one stem. Many of the species are still plentiful and usually more dainty than the hybrids.

The plants are evergreen, and do not produce pseudobulbs. New growths are made each year from the base of the previous growth. The flower stem comes from the centre of a mature growth.

The species can be found all over the old world in the Far East to Thailand and the Philippines, New Guinea and Malaysia. The green-leaved types are cool-growing, whereas those with mottled foliage are the intermediate varieties. They are partly epiphytic and partly terrestrial, but in cultivation they like shady, moist conditions. Good house plants, they do even better grown in an indoor case. Paphiopedilums should be kept watered all year. They have varying flowering times and can bloom at any time. The blooms are extremely long-lasting from eight to ten weeks.

Pictured above is *Paphiopedilum* Western Horizon.

Wilsonaras are one of many hybrid genera which owe their existence to the skills of the hybridists. Wilsonaras are created by crossing *Oncidium* with *Odontioda*. This crossing of genera works extremely well in orchids, to an extent which is possible in no other plant group. The sub-tribe Oncidiinae, which contains odontoglossums and many other natural genera, will interbreed with great ease to produce robust plants which seem to have a tremendous vigour. Whether in a greenhouse or on a windowsill, they will thrive given the very basic requirements. Many of them are 'heat tolerant' and appear equally at home in temperatures much too high for their true *Odontoglossum* ancestors.

It is little wonder, then, that *Odontoglossum* intergeneric hybrids have become more popular than the natural genus, with all its attendant problems of culture. Hybrids such as vuylstekearas, odontocidiums, odontiodas, banfieldaras and many others have given rise to a fantastic range of colourful plants which cannot be equalled in versatility. Most will flower on very young plants, three or four years old. Each following year sees more flowers as the plants reach maturity. Due to their mixed pedigree, most complete their pseudobulb within nine months and bloom regardless of the time of the year. This can mean flowers every nine months, with the plant blooming at a different time each year. Shown above is *Wilsonara* Tigertalk 'Beacon' AM/RHS.

Another group from which many hybrid genera have been produced is the sub-tribe Laeliniiae. This includes the natural genera of *Cattleya, Laelia* and *Brassavola* among others. All these interbreed with such ease, and so many hybrids have been raised, that there are more intergeneric than specific hybrids. While the species dwindle and become ever more scarce, the hybrids multiply in their hundreds each year, and the hybridising becomes ever more complex. The beauty of these intergeneric hybrids is undeniable. The colours have been increased to encompass all shades from pure white to vibrant purples. Again we see an unmistakeable vigour bred into the plant from so many generations of line breeding. The modern *Laeliocatt-leya* or *Brassolaeliocattleya* hybrid is a living testament to the hybridiser's art.

They require intemediate greenhouse conditions where possible, but will also succeed in a warm, sunny room or sun lounge. They require plenty of light, without strong sunlight, and most have a resting period for part of the winter. Their pseudobulbs are tall and club-shaped; their flowers appear, usually from inside a sheath from the apex of the pseudobulb which may carry one or two thick fleshy leaves. Their root system is extensive and can become aerial when the plant grows over the edge of its pot. The flowers can be 6 in (15 cm) across, very softly textured, and last for up to three weeks in perfection. These are the largest of the more commonly grown orchids in cultivation.

These hybrids originated from epiphytic species which inhabited the vast tracts of virgin jungle from central South America. Above is shown *Laeliocattleya* Danaris 'La Tuilerie'.

This *Oncidium chrysodipterum* 'Burnham' is an example of a rare and unusual species, which would undoubtedly be extremely popular if only it were generally available. It would appear always to have been scarce, even in its native Colombia. There are no reports of this plant being shipped by the thousands to astonish and delight the earliest orchid growers. There are no records of high prices being paid for the first specimen. Indeed, this species was discovered very late in the nineteenth century, and was not seen in flower until 1891. To the best of our knowledge it has received little recognition from various authorities by way of awards. Neither has it been touched by the hybridists. The raising of the species from seed has also proved difficult.

The plant belongs to a small select group of oncidiums, sometimes placed into a separate genus, *Cyrtochilum*, all of which have club-shaped sepals with a characteristic small lip. They all produce trailing flower spikes up to 12 ft (4 m) long on a mature plant. The 3 in (8 cm) flowers are born on short side branches with two to four on a branch.

This species is a high-altitude plant found growing epiphytically in the Andes. The few plants in cultivation succeed in a cool airy greenhouse with conditions as similar as possible to the homeland. Its specific name means literally 'golden wings' and refers to the two lateral petals which are golden yellow spotted with brown.

Orchids become rare for various reasons; the overcollecting of natural colonies and destruction of the habitat are the most common reasons, to which can be added the difficulty to grow or flower in cultivation.

This *Encyclia cochleata* flower is certainly not typical of an orchid flower although it is typical of its group within the genus and therefore not unusual. *Encyclia* contains many examples of these 'upside down' flowers, where the lip is seen at the top of the flower and the sepals and petals are held below. These are called non-respinate flowers, as they do not turn to bring their lip on the lower plane as do most orchids. There is presumably some advantage in this for the pollination of these flowers.

Encyclia cochleata was the first tropical orchid to flower in Great Britain. It did so in 1786 at The Royal Botanic Gardens, Kew.

There are very few hybrids within *Encyclia* which is still dominated by its species, many of which are extremely pretty, highly fragrant, or both, and certainly all worthy of being grown. They are mostly cool house orchids, which adapt well to indoor culture, as does this species. It is a native of South America where it grows as an epiphyte. Fortunately, along with others of its genus, it remains fairly common today. It also propagates easily from backbulbs and seems to relish living in cultivation.

When mature, the club-shaped pseudobulbs topped by two leaves can produce a flower spike which will continue to produce a succession of blooms lasting for twelve months or more. At this stage it becomes perpetually blooming.

The most popular orchids are undoubtedly the more showy types. Although the number of these is huge, there are, nevertheless, far more species which are less showy and held to be of lesser interest to the average orchid grower.

There exist among the species many which are totally miniature. The plants often less than 1 in (2.5 cm) high have minute flowers, some not much bigger than a pin's head; others, with foliage several inches high, carry flowers half the size of a thumbnail. In this miniature world can be found the same diversity as amongst the larger orchids. Their beauty is appreciated best by the use of a magnifying glass. As amongst the larger orchids there are those which mimic bees, butterflies and other insects, so in the miniature varieties can be found mimicry of the smaller insects, beetles, ants and so on. The genus *Pleurothallis* is typical of this. It is a large genus, often overlooked, but fascinating when the beautiful or sometimes bizarre minute flowers are examined.

Pleurothallis pubescens (above) illustrates this type of flower. The strange, beetle-like brownish flowers 'sit' on the surface of the leaf. The flower stem emerges from the base of the solitary leaf, supported by a thin basal stem. These intriguing little flowers can be every bit as rewarding to grow as the larger specimens. In cultivation they need quite cool, but airy, conditions where they grow with great ease, quickly building up into clumps of good size.

Not all the bizarre orchid flowers appear in miniature. Among the larger flowering varieties can be found some very curious flowers and methods of flowering. The genus *Stanhopea* is known for its highly individually styled flowers. In all the species the petals and sepals are drawn or folded back to totally expose the lip. This lip is a strange adaption; it has two 'horns' which present a wide opening to the pollinating insect which is guided by these extreme measures along the right path for pollinating. The lip is thick and fleshy with a shiny surface. The species illustrated is *S. ecornuta*.

The genus is mostly native to Central and South America, with a few species in Trinidad. They are epiphytic on the branches of trees and their flower spikes are completely pendulous. In cultivation, where they grow and flower with great ease, in a cool or intermediate greenhouse, they are grown in open hanging baskets to allow their flower spikes to grow downward through the basket.

Their flowers are among the most short-lived of all the cultivated orchids, lasting from three days to barely a week. Nevertheless, a large specimen producing a succession of flower spikes can be in flower on and off for several weeks. Added to this they are highly fragrant.

The species are grown, and these are mostly plentiful in cultivation. Hybrids are rare, and not in general cultivation.

The plants have oval ribbed pseudobulbs with a solitary wide, leathery leaf. They are evergreen, the occasional leaf being shed from the back of the plant every other year or so.

ORCHID TYPES

Sympodial orchids are those which start each new growth from the base of the previous one, and so on in a theoretically unending annual cycle. They cannot die, but they can be killed! In their natural habitat orchids have been found consisting of hundreds of pseudobulbs, all on one plant many years old! One, two or more new growths can be made in one growing season. Pseudobulbs (or false bulbs) are so called because they do not grow under the ground, and unlike the true bulb of an onion (left, above) the pseudobulb is more like a potato (below). Pseudobulbs are swollen stems which hold the reserves of moisture for the plant and enable it to withstand quite severe periods of drought. Some may be covered on the outside by the bracts which carry the leaves; others will be perfectly clean from bracts and are green and fresh-looking for many years; others have a protective bract which will remain green until the pseudobulb has matured, when the bract shrivels and dies.

The size and shape of pseudobulbs varies tremendously. It may be squat and round, pear-shaped, club-shaped, or extremely thin and elongated. All perform the same task, and nearly all work as a combined unit to maintain the strength of the plant. If cut up into individual pseudobulbs the strength of the plant has been lost. Each may well produce new growth, but it will be several years before the plant regains sufficient strength to produce flowers. A healthy plant, therefore, will consist of a number of pseudobulbs, some in leaf and some out of leaf. The oldest pseudobulbs will have lost their foliage and the younger bulbs will carry the leaves. The youngest pseudobulb is at the 'front' of the plant, and this will more often carry the season's flowers. In most genera, only at the time of maturity is the pseudobulb capable of producing flowers. If a new growth is made without flowering, the responsibility to bloom passes to the next pseudobulb to be made. There are a few exceptions to this rule. It is possible on young plants to see the progress made over the years from the smallest seedling pseudobulb, with each one becoming larger until the final flowering size is reached.

If the reverse is noted and the plant exhibits small pseudobulbs at the front then the plant is not progressing as it should and the leading pseudobulbs will be incapable of flowering, indicating that a change of culture is required. Sick plants which have more pseudobulbs out of leaf than in leaf must be reduced in size, and the unwanted leafless pseudobulbs removed.

The pseudobulbs are the most permanent part of the plant. Leaves and roots will be formed and eventually die, but the pseudobulbs will outlive them both. Provided the pseudobulbs remain alive even a sick plant will regain its health in time.

The pseudobulbs should always appear plump, an indication that sufficient water is being received. Some species will shrivel slightly during their resting period and this must be allowed to a certain extent if flowering is to follow. The pseudobulbs of some orchids such as calanthes, pleiones and thunias are short-lived; they last only into their second year before shrivelling and their leaves are retained for about nine months only. Other orchids which lose their leaves after one season's growth but retain their pseudobulbs for many years are the lycastes and anguloas.

The evergreen orchids which make up the majority of plants in an average collection have a similar cycle of growing and resting to the deciduous types, albeit less dramatic for the plant. After a pseudobulb has matured there is usually a short period of rest before growth is resumed, and flowering may take place during this otherwise inactive period. If any new growth at all can be seen on the front of the plant and has visibly grown within a week, the plant can be said to be 'in growth'. Only when the new growth has developed a completed pseudobulb does the plant rest. This rest period may be for a few short weeks, requiring no alteration in the watering programme, or it may extend into several months when all or most water is withheld as the plant needs no nourishment and expends very little energy. Our illustration shows two similar plants. The only difference is that the plant on the right is showing a new growth and has therefore experienced a relatively short period of rest. It has gone straight into the production of a further new growth and has therefore not flowered from the leading pseudobulb. This pseudobulb will not now bloom and it will be another nine months or so before the plant will bloom from the new growth. The plant on the left is in flower spike. This has grown from the base of the leading pseudobulb, and while involved with producing flowers the plant will not commence new growth. This will not appear until the blooms have finished or been cut from the plant.

A number of orchid species grow downwards. These are mostly epiphytes whose pseudobulbs, or their leaves, cannot support themselves in an upright position. This is not always true, however, as can be seen here with *Encyclia citrina* growing in a pendent position. This species must always be grown in this natural fashion, and when it blooms from the apex of the pseudobulb, the usually single, large and heavy flower will lack the necessary support to hold itself erect. It will droop vertically, hiding most of its beauty, although not its fragrance, carefully shielded between the two bluey-green leaves.

There are other advantages for these plants. Moisture will run swiftly from the leaves, eliminating the dangers of water remaining inside young growths, and at the same time ensuring swift and perfect drainage. This one aspect is of the greatest importance to *Encyclia citrina*, which is a plant which likes to be kept on the dry side at all times. It should have a crisp, dry look. It will often be found that these pendent 'dry growers' make meagre root systems. Not for them the vast evergrowing mass of splendid white roots, extending to something over a metre; rather, a few solitary roots will emerge carefully, gripping tightly to the bark surface, and growing slowly, never straying far from their basic support. Phalaenopsis are an example of plants which, even when growing in a pot, are continually endeavouring to turn themselves 'upside down'.

A pendent habit to ensure swift drying out; a few meagre roots to sustain life; a sideways rounding of the leaf to retain what little moisture is available; and we have the perfect solution for a plant which exists in a hot, dry climate. By these modifications the plant has adapted to an environment which other orchids would find disastrous.

Our illustration (left) shows a plant of the species *Brassavola cucullata*: the pseudobulbs have been reduced to such an extent they are barely visible, and are stem-like in appearance, being short, and thinner than a pencil. The terete (cylindrical and tapering) leaves, on the other hand, are long by comparison and have become much fattened. They will snap like a young carrot if mishandled. These fleshy leaves have taken over from the pseudobulbs as being the main food store of the plant. For this reason, they remain on the plant for many years, and it is only occasionally that a single old leaf will die. Should some calamity overtake this plant and cause all the leaves to die, the plant will have no chance of recovery.

Terete-leaved orchids can be grown for many years with very little disturbance and without needing any division.

Dendrobium infundibulum (above) is an example of those orchids which cover their pseudobulbs with short, dense hairs. These small hairs are protection from frost, to which the plant is subject in its natural state. They prevent water vapour from collecting on the surface. They are also bristly and must greatly deter marauding pests. This type of protection can also be found on the flower stems of most paphiopedilums and a few masdevallias.

LEAVES

The leaves of all orchids are expendable; they come and they go. Produced to convert sunlight into energy, they are the powerhouse of the plant without which the process of photosynthesis could not take place. Their range and adaptation is infinite, and there are as many variations in the size, shape and structure of the leaves of orchids as there are species themselves.

From a leaf, everything can be learned about the plant supported by it. The condition and health of the plant can be ascertained by the feel of the leaf; it should be cool and firm to the touch, never limp. The colour is also important, and, although this can vary through many shades of green, an unhealthy yellow green is usually a sign of ill health and lack of food. For one reason or another the plant is starving and in need of repotting, and, a little later, feeding to bring back the healthy colour. Leaves may be highly glossed, or matt finished, self-coloured, or mottled in green and grey patterning. Depending upon their life span they may be soft and papery, designed to last for just one growing season before being shed; or hard and solid, capable of living for many years, sustaining the plant through many seasons, often becoming scarred and marked with age. Their appearance is an indication as to whether the plant prefers strong light or shadow. A hard, dark green leaf will take exposure to sunlight without coming to any harm, and indeed sunlight is

beneficial to the flowering of that plant, whereas a delicate soft leaf will prefer the shade, and will be easily burnt if exposed to direct sunlight. Where large pseudobulbs exist on a plant, the leaves will, more often than not, be considerably light and thin. Smaller, almost non-existent, pseudobulbs will require heavier, more fleshy leaves to compensate. A pseudobulb may support a solitary leaf, or numerous leaves, as illustrated. This picture shows the gigantic *Grammato-phyllum wallisii* 'Burnham' FCC/CCC/RHS, one of the largest species in the world, the long sugarcane-like pseudobulbs flanked for most of their length by huge leaves.

Many orchids, the terrestrial species, do not possess pseudobulbs and compensate with underground tubers. Only the leaves and flowering parts are visible above ground, these usually being of annual duration.

Leaves may be discarded by the plant one by one, at a time prior to winter resting, or later, at the start of the new growing season. Alternatively, all leaves may be shed at one time, thus allowing a complete resting period.

The softer the leaf, the more susceptible it is to insect pests. The very tough leathery leaves seem immune to most sucking pests such as red spider mite.

Paphiopedilums are sympodial orchids without pseudobulbs. They produce growths consisting of three or four leaves each. Commencing with a single seedling growth, the plant makes further independent growths, each one gaining in size until maturity is reached, a process which will take four or five years. Each growth matures and blooms from its centre before the next commences from the base of the previous growth. It is always the most recently-formed growth which carries the flower and once it has flowered a growth will not bloom again. Like an ageing pseudobulb it becomes a food store. For this reason a plant of several growths is kept as one unit, and not divided into single growths!

There are two distinct types of *Paphiopedilum*. These are the plain, or green-leaved, varieties, and the mottled-leaved varieties (above). The latter exhibit a tremendous variation between species and into the hybrids, where further intermediate patterns are formed.

Those with a chequerboard effect of light and dark green areas following the veins of the leaf are among the most beautiful of any orchid foliage. Others are distinctly marbled. This mottling of the upper surface is an indication that the plant is shade-loving and often requires more warmth than the coolest orchids – an average temperature of 18°C (60°F).

Paphiopedilums are evergreens, although in their natural state certain species such as *P. bellatulum* become deciduous while coping with harsh conditions. In cultivation leaves last for several years before being discarded, one growth at a time.

The beautiful mottling on the leaf surface is not the only attraction of *Paphiopedilum* leaves. The base of the plant as well as the undersides of the leaves can be peppered with dark purple. This dark colouration around the base is not a cause for concern: it is in fact a sign of good health. It is also an indication of a dark-coloured flower, and is never seen in green- or yellow-flowered paphiopedilums. However, it is seen in the white-flowered species such as *P. bellatulum* and *P. niveum* which belong to a different group. *P. venustum* is an example of a mottled-leaved species which is totally purple on the undersides of its leaves. Such species are mostly terrestrial, adapted to growing in grassland or woodland areas where their bases are to be found partially buried amongst the low-growing mosses or forest litter. In this way the base of the plant is obscured from the sunlight, and has therefore evolved with non-chlorophyll-making cells.

This colouration can be found elsewhere, in particular among the tall-growing, two-leaved *Cattleya* species known as the bifoliate cattleyas. Here, the purple shows up clearly on new growth, but is gradually lost. It may appear on the leaf's upper surface and on the new sheaths protecting the growing pseudobulb. *Odontoglossum grande* covers the undersides of its leaves with delicate brown flecking, and many other examples may be found.

The green-leaved paphiopedilums carry none of the colourful adornments in the form of rich mottling. They also have much glossier foliage, their leaves being long and fleshy. They can be extremely brittle and are all too easily cracked if roughly handled. Many of these species grow wild epiphytically in the lower branches of trees, or lithophytically on rocks, and are often subjected to periods of drought when their fleshy leaves hold sufficient reserves of water to sustain them. The harsh terrain will take its toll on the wild population whose leaves suffer as a result. The cultivated plant, on the other hand, has never looked so good, watered evenly and regularly throughout the year. With no enforced rest and no resulting stress to the plant, they become the most beautiful specimens under care, exhibiting their luxuriant clean foliage which is a joy in itself. The flowering of such plants comes as an extra bonus!

The green-leaved species which originate from the far east can be grown in a cool, shady situation. The larger, more fleshy varieties from the Philippine Islands and Malaysian Peninsula require warmer conditions, also with good shade.

Very few pests will attack these orchids, which are among the cleanest to grow.

Phalaenopsis are monopodial, growing continually from the centre. Being bulbless, the leaves are succulent, broad and flat. Some species can have leaves a mere 1 in (2.5 cm) in length, such as *P. lobbii*, whereas the largest of the species, *P. gigantea*, produces leaves 12 in (30 cm) wide. The plants grow in deep shade and the leaves are extremely sensitive to light, water and extremes in temperature. Although warm-growing (a minimum temperature of 18°C, 65°F, suits them) the wide leaves will easily burn if exposed to direct sunlight.

Their natural habit is to hang almost horizontally on the trunks of trees, forming a bracket at right angles to the tree. If grown upright they are continually striving to turn themselves over. They can either be straightened at repotting, or allowed to hang over the side of the pot.

Phalaenopsis will produce one new leaf per year, flowering in between. If a plant blooms from more than one stem without making a new leaf, it may be necessary to remove the flowering stem to allow further growth. An average healthy plant will consist of no more than five or six leaves, and should lose no more than one per year. Phalaenopsis can rot from the centre if affected by cold or water lodging in the growth, and when this happens the whole plant may be lost. Occasionally, when all leaves are lost, if the rhizome or crown of the plant is undamaged, new growth may start there. Because of the dangers of rotting, the leaves are better kept dry at all times.

The leaves of phalaenopsis are extremely beautiful and can be plain green or mottled with grey or light and dark green.

The monopodials are a large group of pseudobulbless orchids which grow continuously from a stem. These plants usually consist of a single upright rhizome with the leaves being produced from the centre. As each new leaf is formed and the plant progresses upwards, the effect is of a single stem bearing leaves from alternative sides. This presents a flat appearance and does not form a rosette. There are many hundreds of different species within dozens of different genera, which are widely distributed from Africa through India, Asia, right across to the Philippines and Australasia. An interesting fact about these plants concerns their leaf tips. Each species is of a different shape, the ends of the leaves having a 'chewed' appearance. This is a natural development and all monopodial leaf tips are serrated to a greater or lesser degree. A skilled orchid grower can identify one species from another merely by its leaf tips. The plant illustrated is *Vanda tricolor* in which the characteristic is very pronounced. The jagged appearance shows clearly the uneven ending of the foliage.

Lockhartias are specialised sympodial orchids without pseudobulbs producing a new growth from the base of the previous one. The elongated stems are clothed in short, flattened leaves, and the blooms appear close to the foliage at intervals between the leaves. This type of growth may resemble a monopodial structure, which it is definitely not. Several non-related orchids have evolved with similar foliage, the short leaves close to the stem being a successful development when coping with harsh conditions. *Lockhartia oerstedii* is a species from Mexico, and this growth habit can also be found in dicheas from Honduras and the monopodial *Angraecum distichum* from East Africa, among others.

The *Lockhartia* stem will continue to extend for several years, flowering as it does so, until maturity is reached. The new growths do not wait for maturity of the previous stem but start growing each spring. The result is a considerably large plant within a few years, with stems up to a yard or metre high. At this stage they will form semi-pendent plants, ideal for growing naturally on a tree branch. It is an evergreen which will lose a few leaves each year from the base of the oldest stems. The delicate, plaited appearance hides a strong interior, and the plant can cope easily with adverse conditions.

In cultivation, this type of foliage can be regularly sprayed with little risk. Such plants do well mounted on bark.

Aeridovanda Mundyii shows the complete adaption of an epiphyte. It can exist with nothing around the roots. It is monopodial and has little reserves of water. The continued existence of the plant is completely reliant upon the foliage, terete leaves which have become completely rounded, thinner than a pencil, their surface reduced to the minimum to prevent overheating and dehydration. No part of the plant is soft, the roots are thin and wiry, the leaves hard, almost rough to the touch. Thus the plant is able to stand a severe climate, at the same time capable of extracting what little moisture there is available through its foliage. Thus the leaves become all important; if these were to be lost the plant would find it very difficult to survive long enough to regrow from the stem. Although beautifully adapted to prevent overheating, this plant would suffer severely from cold, and could not withstand exposure to frost. It is known, however, that some terete-leaved orchids are capable of withstanding frost, and some often do, in their natural environment. *Brassavola nodosa* is such a plant.

The dendrobiums comprise an enormous genus and their growth is extremely varied to suit all environments. A somewhat unusual species is *D. cunninghami*, which is adapted to the temperate conditions of New Zealand. The more typical elongated but plump pseudobulbs have here been reduced to thin stems which branch and rebranch, each stem clothed in thin, narrow leaves until the whole plant becomes a loose bundle of stems and leaves. Lacking the rigidity to grow upright the plant forms a pendent green shower, ideally fitted to a cooler climate which experiences high winds. In cultivation it is ideally suited to culture on bark. Occasionally losing a few leaves, which are not missed, it is an evergreen which can be regularly sprayed throughout the year, and not given the completely dry resting period of the Asian species. The thin, diminutive pseudobulbs carry little food reserves and would not sustain the plant through any lengthy period of drought, although in extreme seasons the soft leaves would quickly be shed to help the plant.

The leaves of *D. cunninghami* are far more important to it than the roots or the pseudobulbs, both of which appear very meagre and limited in their usefulness to the plant.

D. cunninghami is not often found in cultivation but it represents an attractive growing habit which is not difficult to cater for in a cool greenhouse.

Aeridovanda is not a natural genus but a hybrid from *Aerides* and *Vanda*. It is also related to the phalaenopsis. These plants will only succeed in cultivation under warm, humid conditions. A moist atmosphere and constant light spraying is most important to their welfare, and a minimum temperature of 18° C, 65° F with good light at all times will suit them. Incorrect culture will result in the rapid loss of leaves which in non-terete specimens would become blotched but survive.

The genus *Vanda* (left) belongs to the large group of monopodials which are widely distributed throughout Africa and the Indian sub-continent, the Far East and Northern Australia. The plants grow by producing a single upright rhizome with leaves on alternate sides. New leaves always come from the top. Flower spikes are produced at regular intervals from the axils of the young leaves. Aerial roots are also made at intervals from the opposite side to the leaf, lower down on the plant. The leaves may extend all the way down the rhizome, or in time, as the lower leaves are shed, a 'leggy' stem is exposed. The stem will retain the roots and more will appear higher up the plant. If the centre of the plant is damaged in any way, new growth will come from the base. Food and moisture is retained in the thick fleshy leaves and roots, enabling the plant to withstand long periods of drought if necessary.

Annoectochilus and related genera comprise a group known collectively as the jewel orchids (above). Undoubtedly theirs is the most beautiful foliage of any in the orchid family. The plants are terrestrial and grow in heavy shade, in warm humid forests throughout the Far East and parts of the USA. They grow from a fleshy horizontal rhizome which lies on the ground. Their plants form a rosette of leaves and bloom from the centre upon maturity of the growth. The glistening beauty of the leaves can be a deep velvety green, copper or mauve, laced with gold or silver threads.

These beautiful orchids do not adapt to cultivation and tend to die even with specialised culture within a few years. Culture in a bell jar is often successful for a while.

There are numerous miniature orchids found throughout the world which deserve more attention. They are every bit as beautiful as their larger counterparts although a magnifying glass is helpful to see this clearly. These tiny plants are mostly all leaves, as can be seen in the top plant (above), *Ornithocephalis iridefolius*. This is a fully mature plant which produces a fan of leaves with the flower spikes in between the leaves. Our lower plant is *Pleurothallis stellis*, a typical member of a large genus which has short stems and single leaves. Both plants come from tropical America. Their small stature is successful wherever there is sufficient moisture for their needs, although many of these tiny plants exist on the very extremities of the thinnest tree branches in what would appear to be very dry conditions. The leaves are responsible for maintaining the plant's store of moisture.

One further adaption in orchids can be found among the epidendrums. The species *E. falcatum* retains all its weight in the thick, heavy leaves (right). The root system is not numerous, but strong enough to hold a heavy plant firmly in its place on a tree. The pseudobulbs are merely short stems which support the long, spear-shaped leaves which, rough and hard, will withstand a harsh environment. They are the main source of food supply for the plant. Only occasionally is a single old leaf shed, their lifespan being for many years. The plant grows from a downward-creeping rhizome and the large green flower emerges from inside the base of the leaf. In cultivation the pendent habit should be retained and regular spraying is essential.

ROOTS

All orchids produce roots. There are basically two kinds: aerial and underground. The root structure of orchids is peculiar to them, and all their roots are of a uniform thickness which does not increase with age. The roots will branch, in some species freely. All consist of a central wiry thread which is surrounded by the fleshy, moisture-retaining, part which in turn is coated by the white papery covering, the velamen, which grows as the root extends, leaving only the green growing tip exposed.

Epiphytic sympodial orchids produce their roots from the base of the leading growth at some stage during the young growth's development, and will give it a tremendous boost with a fresh food supply. In cultivation these roots can be aerial or underground depending upon the angle at which they are produced. Some may grow horizontally and remain as aerial roots until they come into contact with compost when they will grow into it to become terrestrial. Roots made directly underneath the new growth will immediately penetrate the compost and either remain there or emerge from the pot at some stage and revert to being aerial roots. If artificially repotted, however, they will immediately suffocate and die, as will underground roots which are suddenly exposed to the air. One type can become the other by growing naturally, but both can be killed by a grower's interference.

Healthy roots are firm, mostly white, silvery in phalaenopsis and brown in paphiopedilums. Dead roots are soft, they may be wet or dry, and the outer covering is easily removed leaving the inner core exposed. Healthy roots can be damaged by pests or accidentally broken. Broken root tips will heal themselves and after a short time will recommence to grow from above the broken end. The life span of a root can be one season only in orchids whose pseudobulbs are of annual duration or the roots may live for several years, their life span related to the state of the pseudobulbs they are supporting. When leaves are eventually shed, that pseudobulb has no further use for roots, and they will die naturally. On dormant roots the growing tip ceases and is completely covered by the velamen. These roots will recommence to grow at the start of the next growing season. Roots can be killed when a plant is being persistently overwatered, or is left standing in water. Roots can be prevented from growing by inappropriate compost, or severe dryness at the wrong time.

Monopodial orchids which grow tall, such as vandas, produce aerial roots from along the rhizome, from a node on the opposite side of a leaf. Here only one root is made and this will extend, rarely branching, for a considerable length. Usually one or two roots will be made each year.

The roots of epiphytic orchids serve the plant by providing the food source for the plant, and adhering to the tree or rock surface holding the plant firmly in place. Aerial roots can survive only where there is no danger of them being frozen. Terrestrial roots are protected by being under the ground.

A small group of orchids consist merely of a small crown from which bursts a mass of tangled roots. These species, among them the genus *Microcoelia*, have roots which produce chlorophyll.

Plants within the genus *Cattleya* and related genera produce some of the most extensive root systems of any orchids (left). Their roots are thick and fleshy, and it is not unusual for a specimen to produce 80 per cent of its root system outside the pot. Roots like this can be fed to great advantage. This plant can be repotted and the roots trimmed to about 6 in (15 cm), or left outside the pot.

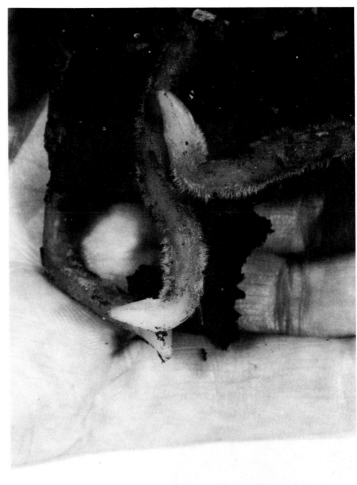

Among the oncidiums are a quite distinct group of bulbless plants whose species originate from the islands of the Caribbean. Long neglected and considered difficult to grow, these highly attractive plants are now gaining in popularity as hybrids are being produced with compact-sized plants and extremely showy blooms. The plants form fans of leaves and when in bloom need be no higher than 12 in (30 cm). Nevertheless their culture remains specialised, and their roots are all important to them. They do not take kindly to pot culture and should be accommodated on bark. Pieces of rough bark are ideal, as their extensive fine root system will take advantage of every crevice, the roots hugging the bark as well as growing freely in the air. Once established, the roots cling very tightly to the bark and the plants should not be disturbed for many years. There is no compost to go stale or require replacing, and therefore no advantage in moving them. An extremely attractive method of growing and displaying these little plants is on a tree branch especially cut for the purpose. It will last many years before finally rotting.

Humidity is extremely important to these cool-growers, but cold and damp must be avoided. The humidity should be in the atmosphere rather than around the plant itself. The base of the plant and surrounding roots should be kept dry. For this reason equitant oncidiums should not be attempted indoors.

The roots on paphiopedilums are quite distinctive, always thick, hairy and brown in appearance. This makes it less obvious to tell live roots from dead ones, but the outer core will easily peel away on any dead roots. Although some paphiopedilums grow epiphytically or lithophytically, they do not produce aerial roots in cultivation, but keep their roots firmly in their pots. Compared with the plants in our previous illustrations, paphiopedilums make a meagre root system, but the few roots that are produced from each growth grow continuously passing on a steady supply of nutrients to the plant, which otherwise have little means of moisture storage. Without pseudobulbs the roots become even more important to the plant, and if they die prematurely the plant will suffer from starvation and dehydration. Therefore underwatering is the great enemy of paphiopedilums.

Paphiopedilums growing in their natural environment produce roots that extend for many feet across the surface of a rock face, taking advantage of any crevices or burrowing into surface mosses or forest litter. In this way they obtain sufficient moisture without the danger of becoming too wet. Species growing terrestrially will push their roots deeper into the ground which will consist mostly of leafmould. When repotting these orchids, little root pruning is necessary, and roots which are not too long may be returned safely to the pot without shortening.

This picture shows two root structures, on the left *Cymbidium devonianum* with fat, healthy roots growing straight down through the compost, an obvious sign of a sweet compost. Note that the roots are all round the edge of the compost ball. This particular plant has been repotted for six months, and this is a young root system growing vigorously and capable of taking up maximum moisture. Such a root system should not be allowed to dry out. *C. devonianum* has dimunitive pseudobulbs and requires these thick roots to ensure a ready supply of moisture, although not all small-bulbed orchids possess thick roots. Within another twelve or eighteen months this root ball will be solid and the plant ready for 'dropping on' into a larger pot. The *Maxillaria praestans* (right) is a fine rooting species whose roots have completely enveloped the ball of compost and is therefore ready for 'dropping on'. The numerous fine roots will take up as much moisture as the thicker roots, but may be potted in a fine grade of bark.

In their natural environment both are epiphytic species; *Cymbidium* roots would be lightly covered by debris in the axils of branches, whereas the roots of the *Maxillaria* would be hanging free below the branch eventually to form a thick mat of truly aerial roots.

In this illustration of *Oncidium sphacelatum* it can clearly be seen how an explosion of new roots erupts from the base of the new growth, but only after the latter is fairly well developed. New roots always follow new growth. It would have greatly benefited this plant had it been repotted before the growth of new roots, which have now developed as aerial roots. The roots if terrestrial would have found more food in the fresh bark than they can do as aerial roots. To repot this plant now would virtually destroy the whole root system, as the roots would be buried in the compost, where they would suffocate and die. Therefore this plant is best left for the season, its aerial roots fed, until the next resting period commences. Repotting can be done at the right time in the spring after the commencement of the next new growth, before any new roots appear. The existing aerial roots can then be trimmed back to within a couple of inches (5 cm).

O. sphacelatum is an epiphytic species which grows well on bark in cultivation, when extra feed can be given during the growing season to enable the plant to produce large pseudobulbs. The aerial roots will live for several years, often until their pseudobulb becomes leafless.

This *Dendrobium pierardii* provides a further example of an epiphytic species producing a crown of aerial roots. These fan out from the base of the new growths in all directions, growing at an extremely fast rate. These very straight roots will continue to extend throughout the summer, often ending up as long as the canes. Their own weight will soon cause them to assume a pendent habit, when they become entangled with the canes, often adhering to and growing along their length. These are annual roots, which serve the plant for one season only. They cease growing as the long caned pseudobulbs reach maturity, to die naturally at the same time as the leaves are shed and the plant prepares for its dormant period. Heavy moisture in the form of air humidity and regular spraying three times a day is necessary for these roots to develop and grow. The roots will not form in a dry atmosphere, and the plant will go through a whole season without their support, relying instead on the older canes to nourish the new growth. This will cause considerable strain on the whole plant. A vigorous plant can be reduced to bare shrivelled canes with death imminent in just two growing seasons if these new roots are not encouraged to grow.

It will therefore be seen that in the culture of the deciduous dendrobiums, whether they be grown in a pot or on bark (and bark is preferable), success depends entirely upon a healthy root system. This is true from the very start, as can be seen where the plant has naturally propagated itself, the propagations on the lower halves of the older, leafless canes showing the same rapid burst of root activity. These propagations should be left on the main plant for twelve months, after which time they can be removed and given their own piece of supporting bark. The roots can remain undisturbed and be used to wire the young plant in position. The next season's roots will quickly adhere to the bark with a firm grip, thus serving the plant in two ways.

Alternatively, the propagations can be left where they are and grown on in this position on the mother plant to form an even bigger specimen overall.

Provided the essential moisture is freely available it is not necessary for these aerial roots actually to be gripping any surface, although it is their natural tendency to do so wherever they come into contact with a surface. Propagations will eventually grip the cane they are growing from, or surrounding canes and even leaves.

There are a number of orchids from different parts of the world which have nothing in common with each other except for the production of a certain type of root. These include the South American stanhopeas, as illustrated, ansellias from East Africa, some species of *Grammatophyllum* from the Philippines, and, alone among the cymbidiums, *Cymbidium traceyanum* from India. In addition to producing a normal root system, when these roots have become fully or partially formed further roots then emerge along their length at right angles to them, they then turn upward and after a short time cease to grow leaving a sharp pointed tip to the end of the root which becomes very hard. Within a few years a dense palisade of short, extremely sharp, pointed roots is formed, with the all-too-clear intention of defending the plant, as can become quickly apparent when the plant is handled and the roots accidentally touched at their tips. Although this is obviously intended to ward off marauding insects or molluscs which could be harmful in the wild, some species of ants find the dense mat of roots an ideal and safe home for themselves and co-habit successfully.

In their natural state these spiky roots will also collect leaves and similar material which will become lodged between them to rot and form a rich food supply for the plant. Under cultivation with plants growing suspended in baskets, as our illustration shows, these roots will, in time, completely obliterate the basket to form a solid protective ball. Although beautiful to look at, this is a problem indeed when repotting becomes necessary; the plant should be handled only with leather gloves!

It should be emphasised here that this fantastic root formation will only be achieved where constant moisture is available to the plant. All too often plants suspended in baskets are allowed to suffer from dryness, due to the awkwardness of regular taking down and dipping, or they simply get forgotten. Added to this, they will dry out quicker in their lofty position hanging in the greenhouse. Again it should be stressed that humidity and moisture are all-important if your plants are to reach their full potential, and every part of them is to be allowed to develop fully.

There is little doubt that the finest orchids are to be grown in a properly controlled greenhouse. However, a greenhouse which is not looked after can become a death trap and certain types of equipment are necessary to ensure that temperatures, humidity and light remain in balance and are suitable for the orchids.

PART II
EQUIPMENT FOR
GREENHOUSE AND HOME

but problems will arise in coaxing them to bloom. Growing orchids indoors is a matter of trial and error. Eventually, it will be found that every plant has a position where it will grow and flower well, and this is the ultimate aim of every indoor grower.

The first essential in any greenhouse where orchids are to be grown is some form of artificial heating. If you are growing only cool-house varieties, heating will be necessary for approximately six months of the year. Intermediate or hot-house orchids will require heating all the year round to maintain the higher temperatures at night. Whatever form of heating is decided upon, it should be more than capable of holding the required temperature without working continuously at full capacity. Also, an additional form of heating should be kept at the ready in case of emergencies when one system may fail.

Having kept the temperature up all winter, most of the summer is spent trying to keep it down, and this is achieved with shading, which will also prevent the plants being burnt by the sun's rays, intensified through the glass.

There are many items of greenhouse equipment which can be beneficial to the orchid grower. For the person who is away from the greenhouse all day, this equipment becomes all the more important, and automation becomes of the upmost importance. Of the numerous aids which are available, we discuss in the following pages those which can be of the most use.

Growing orchids in the home is by far the most economical way, and there is no special equipment needed, and very few additional expenses once you have purchased your orchids. It can also have its rewards and advantages; the plants are always near to hand and can be constantly admired and viewed by visitors without necessitating a visit to the greenhouse. Being under constant supervision, any problems will be spotted quicker, as well as anything that may be a sign of poor health. You will also be quicker to notice when a plant is in need of water, and so on. It follows that the observant grower can attend to the needs of their plants the moment they arise, and has therefore a better chance of growing good plants.

However, in the home, comfortable as it may be, conditions are far more artificial than in the greenhouse, and the plants need to adapt to a much drier environment with less light in most cases. Many orchids will adapt, and this can become noticeable in the colour of the leaves and pseudobulbs, the permanence of aerial roots, as also the length of flower spike, and sometimes the colouring of the flowers. All these aspects can be changed by the environment in which the orchid is growing. Sometimes this can be to the plant's good, sometimes not. Occasionally, beautiful plants will be grown,

Not all orchids are suitable for indoor culture. For some there is not enough light, for others insufficient heat or humidity. Those orchids which will succeed best are the shade-loving, or low-light, types. These include the paphiopedilums, some of the intergeneric odontoglossums, miltonias, and in the warmer range the phalaenopsis. Medium-light plants for the brighter windowsills include encyclias, coelogynes, some dendrobiums, cattleyas, some laelias, maxillarias, odontoglossums, oncidiums, lycastes and many more. It is the high-light, or sun-loving and usually warm-growing, orchids which should be avoided. These include vandas, ascocendas, warm-growing oncidiums, angraecums etc. It is sad that many very young *Vanda* seedlings are brought into this country from Thailand to be grown as house plants. These tiny plants, still in their sealed bottles to meet health regulations, are doomed to die for lack of warmth, humidity and sun. Vandas are a specialist's orchid, requiring the best greenhouse conditions, and have no place in the home.

To achieve the best of both worlds, many growers like to cultivate their young plants in the greenhouse, and as these mature or come into bloom they are brought indoors. By rotating the orchids between the home and greenhouse you can ensure a constant display of flowers throughout the year.

Young plants are not always suitable for growing on indoors; as with all young life, more attention to detail is required, and very young plants will be less likely to adapt without coming to harm.

The ultimate achievement is to see your orchids in full bloom displayed to their best advantage in pleasant surroundings. If your greenhouse is some distance from home, you can bring the plants indoors to enjoy them throughout their flowering time. However, where the orchids are to be grown indoors all the year round it will require a little more than just placing the plants on display. Priory orchid cases are specifically designed for this purpose and are becoming more and more popular. Our illustration shows a beautiful piece of furniture, tailor-made to fit the room in which it is displayed. The orchids live behind plate glass in an environment where the humidity, light and temperature are all controlled. A time clock measures the difference between night and day to ensure that the plants receive the right amount of artificial light every twenty-four hours and that the temperature rises and falls in sequence with the lights. Under these conditions warm-growing, shade-loving orchids such as phalaenopsis and paphiopedilums thrive, producing a beautiful and permanent display which is a feature of the room.

The heater is the most important single piece of equipment in the orchid house. The choice of equipment is wide, from the old-fashioned coal or coke fired boilers with hot water pipes, which can be fired by gas, either bottled or mains, or oil from a reservoir tank to the most modern, clean and efficient electric heaters. The main benefit of a hot water system is that if anything goes wrong, and the fire goes out, you are left with a large reserve of hot water which will keep hot for many hours giving time to rectify the fault. Although reliable, this equipment is expensive to install. The most popular form of heating is by electricity, either tubular, fitted along the walls beneath the staging, or the electric fan heater usually placed on the floor. This produces a current of warm air which circulates evenly throughout the greenhouse, thus ensuring that there are no cold spots. With their built-in thermostats these heaters ensure that the minimum temperatures required are strictly adhered to. There is no waste of fuel that can occur during periods of changeable weather. Gas or paraffin hot air heaters which burn within the greenhouse are also amongst the more popular forms of heating. Cheap and easy to install, they are efficient producers of heat. However, if the greenhouse is well lined with polythene to produce 100 per cent insulation, this open flame heating can produce toxic fumes. These will be detrimental to the plants, especially flower buds and young spikes which can turn yellow in a few days and drop off as a direct result of the fumes from these heaters. To prevent this, ensure that some bottom ventilation is given to supply fresh air. One ventilator on the ridge of the greenhouse should be left open about an inch (2.5 cm) to ensure some fresh air circulation. Whatever main heating is chosen, be certain that it is capable of keeping the minimum temperature required on the coldest of winter nights. Manufacturers of heating appliances will tell you the degree of lift their equipment will offer to the outside temperature. However, the best system can break down and an electricity failure will render even the most excellent of fan heaters useless. It is therefore essential to have more than one type of heating system, and the duplicate should always be different to the main appliance. A paraffin heater which works independently will make a good standby system to be used on a cold night should the mains fail.

Where it is possible run an extra radiator off the domestic hot water central heating system. This can be controlled by its own valves and thermostat making little difference to the overall cost of fuel. The early orchid growers segregated their greenhouses by giving them such fascinating names as the Stove House, the Temperate House and even the East India House. Today they are divided into three simple categories; cool, intermediate and hot. The following chart gives recommended minimum temperatures.

	Cool house		Intermediate		Hot house	
	Day	Night	Day	Night	Day	Night
Winter	16–18°C 60–65°F	10–13°C 50–55°F	18–21°C 65–70°F	13–16°C 55–60°F	21–24°C 70–75°F	18–20°C 65–70°F
Summer	16–27°C 60–80°F	10–13°C 50–55°F	21–27°C 70–80°F	16–18°C 60–65°F	24–30°C 75–85°F	21–24°C 70–75°F

However adequate your heating and ventilating systems they will require monitoring to some extent. It is essential to have a good maximum and minimum thermometer, preferably one that shows the temperature in both Centigrade and Fahrenheit. Many books use just one or the other. Check the thermometer once a day, reset the needles and record in a diary the maximum and minimum temperatures for the last twenty-four hours. It is also a good idea to have an outside maximum and minimum thermometer, preferably placed on a north-facing wall where it cannot be influenced by direct sunlight. Over the years such records will prove invaluable for checking the seasonal variation from year to year against the growth and productivity of the orchids. It can also help to make a few notes about the weather, e.g. sunny, dry, wet or cloudy, against the temperatures. A cross check can also be kept between the thermometer and the thermostat on the heater, making sure both are working properly. Thermostats are notoriously inaccurate and may have variations of several degrees. When this is discovered it is essential to ensure that the recommended temperatures are maintained. As with the outside thermometer, the one inside the greenhouse should not be hung in direct sunlight nor in the path of a fan heater. You need to record as accurately as possible the temperature in the house, particularly around the orchids.

Safety in pest control often causes concern, both on one's own and one's plants' behalf. Therefore, to use a method which automatically controls the amount of insecticide dispensed in the greenhouse always has an advantage. Apart from mixing your own insecticide and spraying the plants, as has been discussed elsewhere, the use of an automatic fumigating system which can be filled with the necessary ingredient is most useful to the grower with a small greenhouse. It gives you an excellent form of control which is not practical in a large commercial nursery. The equipment consists of a small electrically heated pot into which the insecticide or fungicide is placed in predetermined amounts. If you find it offensive when working near it, you have only to switch off the equipment for the time you are in the greenhouse. It need be used only during periods of pest control or as a precautionary measure. This method of pest control is only efficient against red spider mite and greenfly. Other insects, particularly those which live in the compost, are much harder to control by this method, as also for example are scale insects which protect themselves with a scaly covering. Neither will it control slugs or snails which need bait or spray to be killed. The automatic dispenser will also control certain fungal infections where a fungicide is installed. The chemicals used should be alternated from time to time to prevent an immunity developing in the pest.

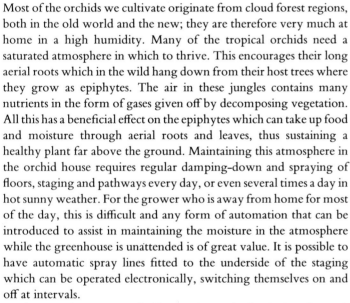

Most of the orchids we cultivate originate from cloud forest regions, both in the old world and the new; they are therefore very much at home in a high humidity. Many of the tropical orchids need a saturated atmosphere in which to thrive. This encourages their long aerial roots which in the wild hang down from their host trees where they grow as epiphytes. The air in these jungles contains many nutrients in the form of gases given off by decomposing vegetation. All this has a beneficial effect on the epiphytes which can take up food and moisture through aerial roots and leaves, thus sustaining a healthy plant far above the ground. Maintaining this atmosphere in the orchid house requires regular damping-down and spraying of floors, staging and pathways every day, or even several times a day in hot sunny weather. For the grower who is away from home for most of the day, this is difficult and any form of automation that can be introduced to assist in maintaining the moisture in the atmosphere while the greenhouse is unattended is of great value. It is possible to have automatic spray lines fitted to the underside of the staging which can be operated electronically, switching themselves on and off at intervals.

The spray line is controlled by an electric 'leaf' which will switch on as soon as the house dries out. This is connected to a humidistat hung on the wall. The most up-to-date method of providing humidity consists of a machine which sends out a continuous spray of vapour, not steam as from a boiling kettle but cool vapour produced by a small fan rotating at high speed and flinging out droplets of water so fine they turn to mist. This humidifex, as it is known, consists of a water container, which holds 2 gallons (9 litres). It needs a daily top-up of water, and no other attention. The same humidifex can be used indoors for house plants. Its original use was to combat the dryness indoors caused by central heating. Models of the humidifex are on the market with at least one firm of orchid sundries stocking them.

Although a humidifex will greatly assist in keeping up the humidity, particularly during the summer months when the humidity is lost through the open ventilators, it is nevertheless no substitute for manual damping-down, which should also be done whenever possible. One humidifex such as illustrated would be sufficient for a 10 × 8 ft (3 × 2.5 m) greenhouse, or one room indoors. It should be placed near the floor, below the plants, to allow the cool vapour to reach the plants standing above.

Within a few weeks of introducing a humidifex into the greenhouse or home you should see a noticeable increase in aerial root activity on your orchids.

In these days of high fuel costs the most expensive item required in running an orchid collection in the northern hemisphere is the heating. Various forms are available as have already been discussed. Prevention of heat loss is the aim of every grower, and insulation of the greenhouse will make a great saving on fuel.

There are two main areas where insulation can be beneficial. One is below the staging level where the greenhouse is built on brick or wooden foundations. This whole area can be lined with polystyrene, polythene or other insulation boards which will withstand the moisture and humidity. Insulating the door and ventilators with any of the proprietary brands of polythene on the market is a necessary step to keep out draughts. If double glazing with glass is used this should have been allowed for in the original construction of the greenhouse. It is much harder to add an extra layer to the inside of your greenhouse after the building has been completed. Glass is a very heavy material and will double the weight on the roof. It should be considered when the greenhouse is designed whether the combined weight of glass and a heavy fall of snow could be borne by the structure. Whatever form of insulation is used you prevent heat loss, but increase the chances of a heavy fall of snow breaking the glass. An extra sharp pitch on the roof is essential if the greenhouse is situated where snowfalls occur often during the winter, in order to make sure that the snow falls off. The most modern methods of double glazing are available for the do-it-yourself orchid grower, and glass double glazing is by no means essential today. There are various grades of polythene sheeting for fixing to the glazing bars with drawings pins or a stapler. For an aluminium house there are specially-designed clips.

A totally sealed greenhouse will give the grower a fresh crop of problems. Condensation will build up on the polythene and reduce the light drastically in the winter when every bit of light is of benefit. Permanent condensation on the polythene will encourage algae to form, thus reducing the light still further. It will also produce a great deal of drip damaging to both plants and blooms. Probably the best method of double glazing therefore is a fine plastic netting which has been put through heated rollers. This seals the weave and prevents fraying. This material can be fixed in the same way as polythene, but because it is full of minute holes it is able to breathe which prevents condensation and drip. Neither does it cut too much light from the plants. The netting is easily obtainable from garden centres. It can be taken down in summer and stored for the following winter. As it does not tear easily, it should last for several seasons.

In a mixed orchid collection such as housed by most amateur growers, plants of all sizes must be catered for and therefore every square inch of space is of some use in the greenhouse. Even the upright ends of the house, as we have discussed, can be covered with trellis or wire netting on which species growing on cork bark slabs can be suspended. Another way of making full use of this otherwise unoccupied space is to buy a quantity of square plastic guttering which makes excellent shelving for low plants in small flower pots. The little plants cannot be knocked off, and the compost will dry out less quickly. Providing that sufficient fall is put on the shelving, there is no danger of excess water collecting in the gutter. As the surplus water will run out of the end it will not harm the plants on the shelf below. Plants housed in this way usually do extremely well as they are easily looked after and there is no danger of the 'one at the back' being missed at watering time. Either north or south ends of the house are suitable, or the guttering can run the full length of the greenhouse at about eye level. Place two thin strips of wood or plastic in the base of the guttering, to raise the pots slightly from the floor and allow a clear run of the surplus water, thus preventing puddles resulting in the plants being saturated.

Nearly all the orchids which we cultivate grow on trees in their natural state. They use the tree as an anchor to climb up from the forest floor to the stronger sunlight and fresh air. To imitate these conditions in our artificial environment we grow the plants in a well-drained and open compost and damp the house to create the humidity which is so essential to the plants. Our cross-section of one pot and its staging pot shows how the moisture given off from the bench is funneled up through the crock hole of the pot taking humidity and moisture to the roots. Because of the well-drained material in which the orchids are growing it is possible for a continuous flow of moist, fresh air to travel up through the compost ventilating the roots well. Here you can see that there is more than one advantage to standing your plants on upturned pots. Before the introduction of the modern plastic pots, growers always used clay pots. In the early days these were all hand-made, providing a rough porous surface to which the roots steadily adhered, and which moisture and air could travel directly through. When plastic pots were introduced the general opinion was that they would be quite unsuitable for orchids; but by changing the conditions and the compost the results were just as good as before, and in many cases better. Certainly good results are easier to achieve with modern materials.

The other advantages of standing your plants on top of pots are obvious. The ones at the back at a higher elevation are easier to see and attend to. Gravel benches are an ideal way of maintaining a moist atmosphere around your plants especially where the benches are made up of sets of plastic trays. These are flooded every day, or if no drain hole is provided in the bench once a week is sufficient. The staging is the furniture in the greenhouse, and it may consist of a series of plastic trays as illustrated, corrugated iron, wood, or similar suitable materials, to give a strong support for the heavy weights which may be placed upon it. There are many different kinds of gravel to cover the bench. We recommend any of the manufactured expanded clay pellets or some form of pumice which can easily be obtained from garden centres. All these hold the moisture well and are easy to wash. Once a year the base material should be removed and washed through a sieve. Add some sterilant to the water which will get rid of spores, slugs etc. If the bench is covered with peat this quickly becomes wet and soggy and will grow unsightly mosses and algae which should not be encouraged.

Galvanised mesh benches constructed on a wooden frame, which has been treated with one of the modern chemicals to prevent the wood from rotting for at least twenty years, makes an ideal form of staging. You have a structure which will last for many years with no attention. The open mesh prevents any collection of rubbish and unwanted algae. This form of staging can be a disadvantage where there is a concrete floor throughout the greenhouse. Maintaining the humidity is going to be a problem, unless a humidifier can be used to create the right atmosphere. Where you have an earth floor with ferns and other ground-cover plants growing, there will be the right atmosphere moving up through the bench around the orchids. The orchids grown on open staging receive the same up-draught effect as a plant standing on an upturned pot deliberately to encourage the movement of moist air.

Capillary matting will keep the whole bench permanently moist, and can be used as a means of keeping moisture around the orchids. However, in view of the open nature of their compost and their swift drainage system, it will not work as a method for watering. A double staging can be used to good advantage, the lower moisture stage covered as previously mentioned, or with the capillary matting, and the open mesh staging above.

If you are not yet in possession of your greenhouse, its selection and the position it is to occupy should be given every consideration. It should not be necessary to hide the greenhouse at the bottom of the garden; the modern well-constructed building can become a feature of the garden adding a pleasing effect to the landscape. Nothing can look smarter than a well-maintained greenhouse in the right place. The choice of houses is unlimited; shapes, sizes and materials to suit all tastes and pockets are available today. The arguments for and against timber or metal will continue for a long time, but generally speaking for orchids, which are a permanent crop and not plants that are planned on a seasonal basis, a timber house will serve better and keep warmer on winter nights. Our illustration shows an unusual structure which has been designed to make the maximum use of the space available. The greenhouse catches as much sunlight as possible and allows the grower inside to reach every plant. This greenhouse, called a Hexalight, is an attractive structure to look at and work in.

It is best to site your greenhouse as near to the dwelling house as possible, thus making it much more convenient to pop out on a cold winter's night to check on the temperature. The other advantage of having the greenhouse near to the home is that the main services such as the water, electricity or gas are cheaper to install. Also, if the home has a hot water central heating system it may be possible to run off an extra radiator with its own controls for little extra cost to the domestic system. When choosing the position for a greenhouse it should be remembered that when it is placed on the north side of the dwelling house or sheltered from the direct sun it will be a much cooler house than one on the south side, but the one on the north will need a great deal more expensive artificial heat in the winter. Generally speaking, we would prefer to site a new greenhouse in a well-lit southerly position providing that it is sheltered from prevailing cold winds. With correct shading and damping the cooling in the summer should not present too much of a problem.

By dividing a section of your greenhouse you can accommodate plants that require different conditions from those grown in the main part of the house. The small section can grow tropical phalaenopsis, and is less expensive than having a separate greenhouse to maintain. The simple method of dividing part of the house with polythene and lining it will provide a box within the environment of the house in which to grow the hotter orchids. The addition of a small, inexpensive heating system will be all that is required. Alternatively, you may wish to propagate or seed-raise your orchids, in which case you will need an area where the higher temperature can be maintained or a propagator which is large enough to be used as a growing case within the greenhouse. Self-contained units as shown in our illustration have their own support system. Thermostats and humidifiers ensure that the day and night temperatures are stable. Phalaenopsis, mottle-leaved paphiopedilums and other less hardy orchids are ideal for these growing cases though some are quite low so you will be restricted to plants that are shorter and more compact. The sliding doors on the front allow the case to be ventilated when the temperature is high enough.

To assist with the propagation of orchids it is not necessary to have expensive equipment as already discussed. It is, of course, beneficial and helps to maintain the right balance of humidity and temperature. A simple seed tray containing various backbulbs and propagations slid inside a polythene bag can be just as effective. One or two bamboo canes placed in the compost of the right length to go from the base of the tray to the top of the bag will keep it in an erect position, forming a tent. This is a simple and effective way of propagating. The polythene bag propagator should not have the neck of the bag completely sealed, to allow for fresh air. The bulbs which have been laid on the compost can be examined at least once a week for signs of activity. Alternatively, you can place your backbulbs in polythene bags, make a few holes for air and hang them up to await signs of growth before potting them up. Backbulbs placed in a tray with compost will benefit from the extra moisture which will encourage the new growth. Orchids will propagate better when confined inside a polythene bag or placed under some kind of cover. It is the warmer and more humid conditions that encourage growth. Cymbidium backbulbs taken for propagating may already be four or five years old, and their spare 'eyes' have lain dormant during this time. It will take some encouragement to activate the 'eyes' and get them growing. As soon as the backbulbs have started to grow and have gained leaves and roots, they can be potted and treated like adult plants. Check also that you have not shut in any uninvited slugs, woodlice, moss flies or other pests that could damage the new growth or 'eye' as soon as it appears. There will be little food for these insects apart from that which you have supplied. A plastic tent can be placed inside the growing case shown opposite which will give even more benefit for propagation as bottom heat can be added.

Orchids grown under glass must be provided with shade. Many orchids grow in full sun in their natural habitat, but it must be remembered that in the tropics where the humidity is high the sun is not always as strong as one would imagine. Also, the orchids grow high in the canopy of the trees as epiphytes where there is a constant movement of air and dappled shade from the branches around them. Although good light under glass will induce them to flower it is important that some form of shading be provided during the spring and summer months. Direct sun with no air movement can easily scorch or even burn foliage. Shading will also protect the house from overheating. The best types of shading are those that are placed on the outside of the glass which cool the greenhouse before the hot rays heat the glass. Blinds fitted internally may shade the plants but will not keep the greenhouse cool though green plastic roller blinds fitted inside can make the plants look very healthy in the artificially produced green light. The best form of greenhouse shading is lath roller blinds fitted to the outside, a few inches from the glass, leaving a space between the blind and the glass to create a circulation of air.

Plastic netting is a most effective form of shading. Some types of plastic netting on the market only have a short life and will last just a year or two before they deteriorate and begin to break up. Those designed specifically for hot climates have a longer life but are more expensive. When used on the greenhouse this net shading is best applied to the outside of the house. A simple form of hooking or clipping the material on prevents it from being blown away. If inconvenient to fit to the outside of the house it may be suspended on the inside from the glazing bars, although this will not keep the greenhouse as cool. Net shading is probably the best for minimum cost and maximum effectiveness. If removed in the autumn and stored carefully it can be replaced in the spring and some will last for many years. The netting will provide enough density for most orchids cultivated. In a mixed collection some plants will require more shade than others. It is therefore best to arrange your orchids so that those requiring full light will be put near to the glass on the southerly side. Shade-loving orchids such as paphiopedilums can be placed behind larger plants, e.g. cymbidiums which can take full light. One plant can be used to shade the other.

The cheapest, quickest and most effective way to shade a greenhouse is with paint shading which can be bought from most garden centres. Apply to the glass by diluting with water and painting on with a large brush. The disadvantages seem to be that you either make the mixture too thick and it is impossible to remove in the autumn or you make it too thin and the first shower of rain washes it off. Another disadvantage is that if you are collecting your own rainwater from the roof the paint may contaminate the water making it unsuitable for watering. Always use the white shading in preference to the green. White will keep the greenhouse cooler and reflect the light. Where the house already has either lath blinds or netting it is a good idea to use the paint shading as well to get into awkward corner and crevices. Often in early spring after a long dark winter we can be surprised by the sudden brightness of the sun. It is the early strong sunlight that does considerable damage to the young new growths. Flower buds can open too early and blooms already out quickly fade and lose their colour. It is important to apply spring shading as early as necessary. Rather than risk damage by early sunlight an emergency protection is to cover plants with sheets of newspaper. This is an operation which takes only a few minutes but will suffice until you have time to apply the permanent shading for the coming summer.

Fresh air is one of the most important items we can give our orchids. Fresh air is free and it is a question of keeping the balance between the supply of air and the temperature in the greenhouse. Opening the ventilators full on a winter's day on the same side as the prevailing wind will lose a great deal of expensive heat and chill the plants. On the other hand fresh air on a hot day will keep the plants cool and help to lower the temperature. We have already seen how important it is to keep the temperature down on summer days with correct damping and shading. Ventilation plays a big part in temperature control. Purpose-built orchid houses are fitted with bottom ventilators as well as top. At the base of the greenhouse, below the staging line, is fitted a 'to and fro' slide which operates manually. It is best left open for most of the summer. To prevent cold draughts, vermin and slugs coming through these bottom ventilators fit a fine gauze galvanised wire mesh over the opening. Used in conjunction with top ventilators this creates a smooth current of air coming in at the bottom and out at the top. Although this may take out some of the atmosphere that has been built up, it will change the air without too much draught. Leaving the door open on sunny hot days may prove adequate ventilation but this will cause a great loss of humidity resulting in watering and damping-down more often.

Many orchids make their home in the wild in the top canopy of huge trees, perhaps 100 feet (30 m) from the forest floor where there is always some movement of air. The movement of air within the greenhouse is greatly assisted by a small electric fan. This fan will keep the air in the greenhouse circulating. Even on dull still days it will have the effect of keeping the atmosphere fresh and buoyant. Where the fan is sited on the floor of the greenhouse this will have the effect of moving the warm air from ground level to the roof and then down again. The small fan, as illustrated, can be left on permanently to keep the air moving at all times. If it causes a distraction, have the switch placed near the door so that when you enter the greenhouse it can be switched off. The whirring sound can become stressful whilst you are working in the greenhouse. Electrical appliances should always be placed where they will not get wet during watering and therefore easily moveable equipment is essential. The effect of a fan will be to dry up surplus moisture quickly, particularly on cold winter days. This eliminates the need to open ventilators for drying purposes. In summer, a tray of water kept in front of the fan will create more moist air. This constant movement will not lower the temperature, although it may *feel* cooler with the fan switched on. It will, however ensure a more even temperature around the greenhouse.

In a small greenhouse the top ventilators are best situated one on each side of the ridge. Most greenhouses run north to south so that the sun covers most of the greenhouse as it passes overhead and maximum advantage is taken of both light and heat available. The ventilators on each side of the house, allow opening of one ventilator on the opposite side from the prevailing wind and prevents direct draughts on to the orchids below. Probably one of the most useful pieces of equipment you can install is an automatic ventilator arm. This is simplicity itself and yet very efficient and accurate in its operation. It works off hydraulic fluid contained in a cylinder which expands with the rising temperature forcing the arm upwards and opening the ventilator. As the temperature drops the fluid contracts and the arm is withdrawn until it is completely closed. This operates at a pre-set temperature which can be adjusted in conjunction with the thermo-meter. Ventilation should always be given in relation to the rising temperature. In a cool greenhouse with a temperature of 50°F (10°C) minimum at night and a day temperature of 60–65°F (16–18°C) ventilation will not be necessary until the temperature has risen above that minimum day temperature of 65°F (18°C). At this point, ventilation on the leeward side may be given. On hot summer days when the temperature could rise as high as 75–80°F (24–27°C) no harm will come to the plants providing that there is adequate ventilation, shade and humidity. It cannot be stressed enough that it is not the importance of ventilation, humidity, light or water alone, but the combination of all these factors which produces ideal growing conditions for the best results from your orchids. In a small greenhouse the temperature can rise with frightening speed. If the temperature is allowed to soar into the 80s°F (higher 20s°C) which it can do in less than half an hour, it will take much longer to reduce that temperature after the ventilators have been opened. Better to open the ventilators early and stabilise the temperature before it goes out of control. During very hot weather, one ventilator can safely be left open all night, thus allowing the rising process in the morning.

By the same token, the closing down or reducing the amount of air in the evening should be done not so early as to cause a sudden rise in temperature, nor too late when the house may have become chilled and take a long time to warm up again. Until you have learnt the behaviour of the greenhouse, always go back to check temper-atures half an hour or so after adjusting them.

ORCHIDS IN THE HOME

Paphiopedilums are the ideal choice for growing indoors. The plants do not produce the usual pseudobulbs but consist of a growth or growths of several leaves alternating to left and right until a flowering stem appears from the centre, which is the culmination of one season's growth. A new growth then commences from the base of the previous growth, and this provides the bloom for the following year. *Paphiopedilum* leaves may be plain green, often highly glossed or marbled or mottled in light and dark green. All are extremely attractive plants when not in bloom. They can be grown into large specimens over a number of years or divided when large enough. Their flowers may be single, or there may be two or more on one stem, depending upon the variety. Their colour range is from white to deep purple with pink, bronze and red in between. Green and yellow are included. The plants are mostly winter-flowering, when the blooms will last for a good eight weeks. If you decide these are the orchids for you, and they are an excellent choice for indoors, with a careful selection of varieties, hybrids and species you can achieve all-year-round flowering.

The plants are compact, and look their best when grown in their plastic pots, placed inside a container which has pebbles or gravel placed at the bottom on which the plants are standing. The base of the plants is level with the rim of the container. The gravel is kept wet, and this allows a certain amount of moisture to rise around the plants while the roots are kept cool. Ideally, the copper trough should be positioned sufficiently close to the window to allow the plants the necessary light, but inside the curtains to ensure that on a cold winter's night there is no danger of the plants getting chilled.

The drawn curtains will afford the plants plenty of protection. The plants in the container can be rotated so that each plant gets a turn at being closest to the window. In this position the plants are well away from any draughts or sources of heat.

Note the leaves on these are plump and shiny, and are quite rigid. This is an indication of good moist conditions at the roots, easily achieved in these surroundings. Drying out is one of the more important points to watch for. These small pots indoors can dry out very quickly, in a matter of hours, and if severely underwatered for any length of time the leaves will lose their gloss and rigid stance to become limp and dehydrated. The remedy is more regular watering and spongeing of the leaves. Excessive dryness will also cause the shrivelling of the bud at an early stage, which after months of waiting can be a disappointing climax.

During the summer months, a window which has plants growing close by can be safely opened for ventilation without harm to the plants. What would be a cold draught in winter becomes a pleasant cool breeze in summer, and is beneficial to the plants. However, a breeze will cause the plants to dry out even more quickly and the water in the container to evaporate.

If this position should prove to be too light, and the leaves take on a yellowing appearance or suffer burn marks, they can be moved back a little way from the window, or net curtaining can be placed against the window for the summer months.

Plants always grow better in groups and orchids are no exception, but where an individual plant is required to be on its own, perhaps as a table centre-piece, it should be placed on a bed of shingle or pebbles topped up with water to give a moist base. A small plant growing in this way must be regularly watered; it will dry out extremely quickly in a bark compost. It can be easily removed to the kitchen for watering and allowed to drain before being returned to its permanent position. This is a good opportunity of giving a light overall spray. With those few precautions the requirements of an orchid are not so different from those of any other house plant, and one orchid plant can make an attractive gift. The recipient who has no previous knowledge of orchids will not go far wrong provided that the plant is kept cool and moist.

Most paphiopedilums will adapt to the fairly constant temperature, but many other orchids will also adapt and can be tried in this way.

Note the signs of good health on the above *Paphiopedilum*. This plant is in a small pot, but quite large enough for its needs. Last year's growth is now carrying a bud, and the new growth which will bloom next year is already showing in front. The mottled leaves are firm and glossy and stand out stiffly from the centre. The common fault with paphiopedilums indoors is limp, dehydrated foliage caused by underwatering or overheating. This condition can arise all too quickly with a combination of a small pot and open, fast-draining bark compost, and the plant in a warm dry room.

A number of cool-growing orchids can be grown on the windowsill close to the glass, to achieve as much light as is available, and behind the curtains, which when drawn will give the plants a small area where the temperature can drop to the low 50s° F (10–12°C). During cold winter nights the curtains can be opened to allow the temperature in the growing area to remain the same as in the rest of the room. The choice of window is important; check the aspect and just how much direct sunlight will be falling on the plants on a hot summer's day. It may be necessary to move the plants from window to window depending upon the season. Remember that although direct sunlight through glass is more likely to scorch a plant than anything else, the plants must receive sufficient light for flowering as well as growing. Fancy pot covers or a single multi-pot-holder will help to keep the roots cool in summer.

The small collection growing on this window ledge are, from left to right, the species *Odontoglossum citrosmum*, the hybrids *Odontocidium* Tigersun and Crowborough, the latter in flower. The tall central plant is the species *Laelia purpurata*, followed by two more species *Trichopilia tortalis* and, in flower, the small and sweetly-scented *Oncidium ornithorynchum*. These are all medium-light plants, and all are ideally suited to this particular window. This group will give a succession of blooming times over the year.

For sheer effect there is nothing to compare with a *Cymbidium* in bloom filling out a corner of the room. Its long, green foliage makes an attractive backdrop to the sprays of flowers and in a cool room a *Cymbidium* will remain in flower for six weeks or more. Standard cymbidiums do not make ideal house plants as they are space-consuming, often requiring 10-in to 12-in (25–30-cm) pots at maturity, and out of bloom require specialised attention, more easily achieved under greenhouse conditions. Nevertheless, they can certainly be brought into the home while in bloom. Miniature cymbidiums, however, are becoming increasingly popular as house plants. Our picture shows a miniature *Cymbidium* in a display area while in bloom. After flowering it should be removed to a south-facing window where the light will be sufficient to harden the plant and to ensure that it blooms year after year.

Even a well-lit windowsill cannot always give sufficient all-round light to a plant the size of a miniature *Cymbidium*. If the plant is found to grow well enough during the summer but does not produce flowers the following season, lack of light is the most probable cause. A further sign of insufficient light would be dark green foliage and pseudobulbs. In this case the plant would benefit from spending the summer out of doors. Cymbidiums which have not bloomed for years and which are otherwise healthy will delight their owner with several years' flower spikes the following season!

Having seen how you can successfully grow orchids as individual plants on the windowsill with no other equipment than a small trough or individual saucers filled with damp gravel, you may now be tempted to look for other forms of container to enclose the plants completely. For example, an old disused fish tank can easily be converted into an ideal place in which to grow a few plants. The glass sides completely enclose the plants and with an inch (2.5 cm) of wet gravel in the base a micro-climate is quickly created and retained. The shorter-growing orchids will thrive in this small community. Choose low-light orchids such as paphiopedilums and phalaenopsis, and then place your container anywhere in the room where it will form a feature. If this is in a dim corner, artificial lighting can be used to increase the light and show the plants off to their best advantage. An angle-poise lamp is ideal for this, or a small strip light can be fixed to the wall behind. Be certain to choose the correct type of bulb, bearing in mind that some lights could cause scorch and permanent damage. A coloured bulb is better than a clear bulb and 60 watts is ample and most effective. The gravel at the bottom of the tank should be checked at regular intervals to make sure that it has not dried out. Just a little water in the base will be sufficient to create humidity around them and to ensure good health. Be careful not to drown them. Although you do not wish to overcrowd your plants it is surprising how many a small container will hold.

There are some places within the home which are quite unsuitable for orchids to be grown. We have seen orchids placed on the mantelpiece over an open fire; this is disastrous and any plant will quickly suffer from heat and dehydration. Keep orchids well away from electrical appliances, and in particular away from the television set which when switched on for many hours at a time will generate hot, dry air. This is apart from the danger aspect of placing a wet container on the set, where if any water were to be spilt into the works consequences could be serious for both the television and the orchid! So keep orchids away from televisions. Orchids should be kept away from all sources of artificial heat. Although central heating is not detrimental and many tropical orchids such as phalaenopsis will thrive in a centrally-heated room, they should always be placed well away from any radiators. A warm draught or constant blast of warm air can kill orchids very quickly. Moisture and humidity are important, hence the humidity trays as mentioned on p. 49. Orchids can be grown in association with other house plants which have proved successful; indeed many house plants are less tough than orchids and are therefore a good guide to the safe places where orchids may be grown.

To be certain of an environment free of warm and cold draughts for your orchids, the ultimate indoor culture is perhaps the indoor growing case as illustrated on p. 32. Here you have near perfect control over every aspect of their growing, and although involving the grower in more expense this is nevertheless minimal compared to the price of an equipped greenhouse.

Orchids in cultivation require regular repotting. An adult plant should be repotted on average every other year, or perhaps once a year, depending upon the type. Repotting should not interrupt the growing cycle of the plant and is therefore best undertaken in the spring, at which time

PART III
POTTING AND
PROPAGATION

of most use to the person who tends to underwater their plants. Gravel or perlite are sometimes included to give an even more open mix which in turn will keep drier. Whatever is added, it should be as durable as the bark. Avoid any rapidly decomposing materials, such as dried bracken.

the new growth is showing, but prior to the commencement of the new roots. When these follow they will grow immediately into the fresh compost taking maximum nourishment from it. Some orchids, particularly the cattleyas and their hybrids, have two growing cycles and will often commence new growth in the autumn, in which case this is also a good time to repot them.

Young plants in small pots will need to be potted or 'dropped' on into larger pots every six months or so, and this also should be done in spring and autumn. The summer growing and winter resting seasons are not good times to disturb orchids and should be avoided.

Repotting becomes necessary when the plant has outgrown its pot, or preferably when it has just filled the pot. Sympodial orchids grow forward, producing each new pseudobulb or growth in front of the previous one. When this reaches the pot rim leaving no room for further growth a larger pot will be necessary. Repotting is also necessary to replace old exhausted compost with fresh, as within two years there is little food value left and more nutrients are required in order for the plant to progress.

The vast majority of orchids in cultivation are epiphytes, or hybrids bred from epiphytic species. It is therefore essential for them to be in a compost which is extremely open and free-draining. The best material to suit their needs is therefore bark chippings, and although different growers favour different composts all are based on bark chippings, which on their own constitute an excellent compost for orchids. This bark is sold by orchid nurseries, and is usually graded pieces of scotch or similar pine, which is obtained from forest trees after felling. Other materials which can be added to the bark include Irish sphagnum peat. This will give a wetter compost and is

Most orchids will be happy in ordinary plastic pots; in fact, these are preferable to clay pots owing to the dry nature of the compost. Clay pots are useful for top-heavy plants, standing the plastic pot inside a slightly larger clay one. Those orchids which persist in making aerial roots can be treated differently; they can be put into hanging baskets, or wired onto a piece of cork bark. Cork bark is best because it takes a very long time to rot and because the roots can easily adhere to the rough surface. An 'orchid tree' with several plants tied to a tree branch can become a most interesting feature in the greenhouse. It is also advantageous to those orchids requiring plenty of light to grow them in this manner where they can be hung close to the glass.

Whereas the propagation of many orchids is easy and rewarding, the raising of orchids from seed is far more complicated and cannot be achieved as easily. Nevertheless, it is not beyond the scope of the amateur grower, and two methods of seed raising are described. Whether you are propagating or seed raising your orchids, both are long-term projects which can take from three to six years to achieve flowering plants.

A further method of propagation is by mass tissue culture known as meristem culture. This is a laboratory technique requiring professional skill and involves the taking of the growing meristem tip from within the new growth, and culturing the nucleus of cells in a similar way to germinating orchid seed artificially. The results are any number of identical plants, all multiplications of the one clone. Only the very finest orchids are treated in this way, making them generally available at reasonable prices.

REPOTTING A *CYMBIDIUM*

This plant has completely filled its pot, and the new growth to the right has no room to develop its pseudobulb. The pot is crammed with roots to such an extent that they are actually pushing the plant above the pot rim. Now, when the growth is a few inches tall, the new roots will start to grow. The plant has four pseudobulbs and one new growth. It is not large enough to be divided, but the leafless pseudobulb on the left can be removed and propagated from if wished. This plant has been dried out for repotting. Remove and retain the label.

The plant is removed from its pot by turning it upside down and sharply tapping the top edge against the potting bench. Tap it well away from the new growth which could be damaged. If the plant does not give, try squeezing the pot or rolling it between the hands and tap again. The pot will be easier to remove if the plant is dry. There will be a solid ball of thick roots. Most of those on the outside will be alive, but the older dead roots inside the root ball should be removed after breaking up the root ball.

The roots are separated by working the fingers into the base of the ball. Eventually, the ball will begin to loosen, and the roots can be eased out to their full length. All old compost will fall away as more and more roots come free. Many dead roots in the centre will just pull away. Some live roots will be broken during this process but they need in any case to be trimmed, so no harm is done. To remove the leafless backbulb take a sharp knife and sever the rhizome between the pseudobulbs, making a vertical cut, and taking care not to slice off the bottom of the pseudobulb.

There should now be no old compost left around the roots, which can be trimmed accordingly. The trimming of live roots avoids broken and damaged roots being left on the plant where they will set up areas of rot. Using a sharp pair of scissors the dead roots, the outer covering of which peels away, should be cut right back to the base of the plant. The live roots should then be cut back to a convenient length of about 6 in (15 cm). When this is done as much as 80 per cent of the original root ball will have been removed. However, to a healthy plant this will not be a setback, and new roots will soon get under way.

The plant is now ready to go into its new pot. It should be given a pot which, when the plant is placed with the oldest pseudobulbs against one side, allows about 2 in (5 cm) of space between the new growth and the pot rim. This will give sufficient growing space for another two years. A plant which has been reduced in size by the removal of backbulbs will often return to the same sized pot. Sufficient crocking material should be used to cover the bottom. Polystyrene pieces of packing material are ideal for this purpose.

A small amount of compost is placed on the crocks, and the plant stands on top of this with its roots carefully folded underneath. At this stage the base of the leading growth should be level with the rim of the pot.

Compost can be added or taken away until the required height is achieved. Note that if the plant is too high it will be unstable, and if too low the high level of compost could cause rotting around the base.

Holding the plant upright with one hand, pour compost in with the other.

As the compost is being poured into the cavity between the plant and pot rim, it should be firmed down with the fingers. There is no need of a potting stick; the bark can be firmed sufficiently with the fingers. Care should be taken to press the compost down around the pot rim, avoiding any direct pressure against the plant. The action of pressing down the compost will lower the plant slightly, taking the base to just below the pot rim. Pressing down can be done with both hands, while the plant sits firmly held by the compost.

The filling in and pressing down of the compost continues until it is level with the base of the plant and the pot rim. It is important to ensure even pressure all round the plant, bearing in mind that there is much more room at the front than to the rear, where it will be a little more difficult to work compost into the small space available. One final pressing down will bring the plant to the same level. Finally, replace the label in the back of the plant. The single backbulb can be potted in a similar way using as small a pot as possible.

REPOTTING A *CATTLEYA*

This is a large plant, which if it had been repotted last year, would not have made so many roots outside the pot. The plant is growing in two directions and new growths can be seen on either side. It is large enough to be divided and will make three plants, two with at least four pseudobulbs and a new growth, and one back propagation, the latter will consist of four pseudobulbs, in leaf, but without a new growth, which will come later. The aerial roots are typical of cattleyas, and these will be trimmed back severely because they will not now adapt to pot culture. New roots from the new growth will quickly make up any loss.

Cattleya roots will adhere strongly to the sides of the pot and can make the removal of the plant quite difficult. If tapping the pot on the edge of the potting bench does not loosen the plant, in order to avoid further unnecessary effort the easiest method is to cut away the plastic pot using a pair of secateurs. Although this will destroy the pot, it will save the plant from any possible harm. A flexible pot is easily peeled, and a rigid pot will break into removable pieces, leaving a solid ball of roots which can then be teased apart.

When the plant has been stripped bare to the roots it can be divided. A leading piece consisting of a double new growth and four-leaved pseudobulbs is removed by severing the rhizome with secateurs. One further leading division of a similar size can be removed from the other side of the plant, leaving a back division with leafed pseudobulbs which can also be potted. Any good leafless pseudo-bulbs should be divided and potted singly. Alternatively the rhizome can be severed in the pot six months before repotting when the back division will have started a new growth.

Having severed the rhizome the divisions will pull apart, revealing a number of dead roots at the centre of the plant. The rhizome which has been cut through is hard and woody, and should come to no harm as a result. However, as a precaution against the possibility of causing a rot to set up in the cut ends, they can be dusted with sulphur or any powdered fungicide to ensure that the areas remain dry. Once the divisions have been separated, any remaining compost will fall away, leaving the bare root divisions ready to be trimmed.

It will be found that the roots belonging to the oldest pseudobulbs will be dead. These roots will have died naturally of old age, and can therefore be removed from the plant. Only those roots supporting the younger pseudobulbs will be alive, and these should be trimmed back to within 6 in (15 cm). The back division of the plant will probably be found to contain no live roots at all, and in this case some of the dead roots should be left on the plant to about 6 in (15 cm) to provide an anchorage when potting the plant.

The divisions are potted according to the usual method as described on page 56, ensuring that the new growth has sufficient room and is sitting on the surface of the compost. Cattleyas should not be overpotted, as can happen due to their long narrow habit of growing. They can be repotted annually, often just 'dropped on' with no disturbance to the root ball. They often need extra support for their top heavy pseudobulbs until new roots have again anchored the plant in its pot. Don't forget extra labels for all the divisions: the date of repotting can also help for future reference.

The staking should be done with a thin bamboo cane inserted into the compost, close to the rhizome at the centre of the plant. Each pseudobulb can be individually tied into place with green garden string. This method of staking controls what can be a most untidy growing plant, and it will be found much easier to accommodate, particularly where a number of cattleyas are to be housed in a comparatively small area.

One month after repotting the *Cattleya* shows vigorous root activity from around the base of the leading pseudobulb. These roots enter immediately into the fresh compost to provide the main source of food for the plant, and the pseudobulbs remain plump and healthy. The advanced new growth behind the leading pseudobulb will produce an even larger pseudobulb and should flower to its full potential as a result. Although supporting canes can be removed once the new root system is formed, the string ties often remain to keep the plant in place.

REPOTTING A *PAPHIOPEDILUM*

Paphiopedilums do not divide as readily as the cymbidiums and cattleyas and although they do not outgrow their pots so fast annual repotting seems to suit them. Certainly the intervals between repotting should not be longer than two years, by which time the compost will have become exhausted. On an annual basis a *Paphiopedilum* can, for a number of years, be repotted back into the same size pot, or, if the compost is still in good condition, be 'dropped on' without disturbance to the root ball, into a slightly larger pot.

A vigorous-growing *Paphiopedilum* can be divided only if there is more than one new growth with at least two mature supporting growths for each division. To reduce the plant further will affect its flowering capability for some years to come. The only reason for dividing paphiopedilums is where they have become too big to manage. Otherwise it is better to keep them as one plant. The rhizome adjoining the growths is quite soft, and the bare-rooted divisions will easily pull apart in the hands.

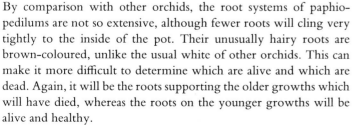

By comparison with other orchids, the root systems of paphio-pedilums are not so extensive, although fewer roots will cling very tightly to the inside of the pot. Their unusually hairy roots are brown-coloured, unlike the usual white of other orchids. This can make it more difficult to determine which are alive and which are dead. Again, it will be the roots supporting the older growths which will have died, whereas the roots on the younger growths will be alive and healthy.

The root trimming on paphiopedilums is all-important, and should be tackled with great care. The dead roots should be felt for, and only removed if they feel flat and empty, with the outer covering peeling away. It will be found that the remaining live roots are less brittle and, therefore, with careful repotting, these can often be left whole, or trimmed only where broken. They should not be trimmed to the same extent as, say, cymbidiums.

Paphiopedilums should be placed into as small a pot as possible, with just sufficient room to hold their roots comfortably. An excess of compost around the roots will quickly lead to overwatering as the roots are confined within a soggy mass containing far more moisture than they can possibly take up. Extra crocking in the base of the pot is an advantage to these plants, in order to ensure the swift drainage so necessary to their welfare. Here, different size pots have been selected for the divisions and ample crocking is being placed in the pots.

Extra attention must be paid to the untrimmed roots to ensure that no damage is caused as they are returned to the pot. The plant should be placed in the centre of the pot, with the roots carefully spread beneath it. As the plant is gently lowered onto the base of compost, the pot can be twisted to allow all the roots to curve around and align themselves one way. This will be found to be the easiest way to handle these longer roots which will settle themselves beneath the plant and around the rim of the pot.

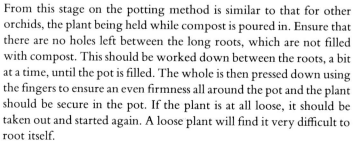

From this stage on the potting method is similar to that for other orchids, the plant being held while compost is poured in. Ensure that there are no holes left between the long roots, which are not filled with compost. This should be worked down between the roots, a bit at a time, until the pot is filled. The whole is then pressed down using the fingers to ensure an even firmness all around the pot and the plant should be secure in the pot. If the plant is at all loose, it should be taken out and started again. A loose plant will find it very difficult to root itself.

When repotting is completed, the divided plants should be sitting centrally in their pots, with the base of the leading growth on a level with the compost. This should be slightly below the rim of the pot, to allow for future watering. Extra labels with the name of plant and date of repotting should be written for the additional plants. For the next few weeks, very careful watering will be required so as to allow any damaged roots to heal. As soon as new root activity is observed around the base of the new growths, normal watering can be resumed.

POTTING IN A BASKET

Orchids can be grown in hanging baskets for a number of reasons. From the plant's point of view it can be of benefit to those which like to receive as much light as possible, as they can be hung close to the glass. It is also an advantage to those orchids which prefer to make aerial roots. From the grower's point of view basket culture can save valuable staging space and it is a good way to accommodate many more orchids in a greenhouse. However, they can create more work for the grower; they will dry out faster in their lofty position and they require more frequent checking to prevent them from becoming too dry. Very often a plant must be taken down to be watered properly and replaced when it has drained. Nevertheless, the little extra attention required by hanging orchids is amply rewarded by their pleasing appearance, and, undoubtedly, their better growth, with resulting improvement in flowering.

Not all orchids are suitable for basket culture; those which do best are the so called 'high-light' plants, those epiphytes which like plenty of light and are grown with minimum shade. These can include dendrobiums, laelias, coelogynes, encyclias, in the cooler sections and vandas and their allies in the hot section. Orchids which would not be suitable include cymbidiums, through their sheer size, excepting the species *C. devonianum* and the 'low-light' or shade-loving orchids such as the cool-growing lycastes and paphio-pedilums, and in the hot section the phalaenopsis.

Orchids growing in a suspended position rely more heavily on a moist atmosphere and basket culture is best confined to a green-house.

Any epiphytic orchid which fits the above requirements can be transferred from a pot into a basket quite easily. There are a number of specialised plastic baskets available for orchids but any container that suits the shape and size of the plant can be used.

Baskets are not always rigid and may have a rounded base, in which case before attempting to pot the plant the basket should be stood inside a slightly larger flower pot to hold it firm and steady. Most types of basket have large gaps between the lattice and must be lined. An ideal type of liner is pea netting which will allow the water to flood through, and young roots to penetrate it easily, while holding the compost in place.

A large square is cut which will be sufficient to line the basket with some overlap at the rim, and placed inside the basket. It is taped into position with lengths of sticky tape which can be removed when potting is completed.

The plant selected is a beautifully shaped *Coelogyne* Burfordense, with three large green pseudobulbs, each topped by a pair of large, broad leaves. This famous old hybrid is an ideal choice with a semi-pendent flower spike of large green, black-lipped flowers.

The *Coelogyne* Burfordense has been removed from its pot and all old compost shaken clear of the root ball. The fine roots needed little trimming, and have now been carefully placed beneath the plant which was placed on a layer of compost in the basket. No crocking is necessary as the basket is perfectly free-draining. The compost is added, a little at a time, taking care not to dislodge the lining, until the basket rim is reached. At this stage the sticky tape can be removed, and the exposed netting around the rim can be tucked in with the points of the scissors to give a neat, finished appearance.

The basket can now be given its supporting wires. For this three lengths of thin wire, preferably the green plastic-coated type, can be twisted into shape with a ring for hanging at the top. The length of the wires, which are fixed to the basket rim, is determined by the height of the leaves. The wire should be slightly longer than the tallest leaf, to allow some clearance from the glass when the plant is suspended. No leaves should be allowed to touch the glass or be so close as to be in danger of getting chilled on a cold winter's night. Ideally, leaves should be no closer than 6 in (15 cm) to the glass.

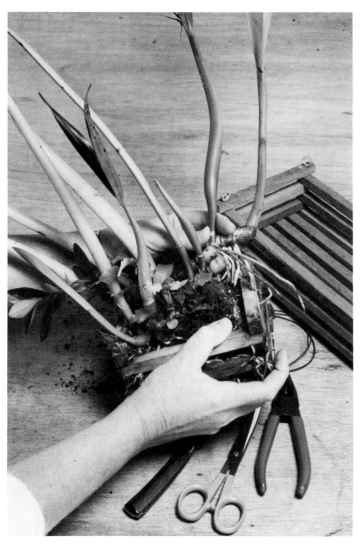

It is surprising how easily a plant which cannot be fitted neatly into a round or square container can be accommodated in a long-shaped basket. These baskets are hand-made especially for orchids, and the handyman can make his own to whatever size or shape is required. The orchids most suited are those which grow forward, usually with a string of pseudobulbs producing a long narrow plant. *Encyclia pentotis* is such a plant. An epiphytic species, it quickly outgrows a conventionally-shaped container at the front, although much space is left around the sides. If this plant were to be repotted using the general guidelines of leaving 2 in (5 cm) of room in front of the leading growth, it would be grossly overpotted with far too much compost and moisture around the roots which would lead directly to overwatering.

Orchids which have been growing in baskets for some length of time will have attached their roots firmly to the wooden slats, and it is difficult to remove the plant without some damage. We have previously seen, however, that these epiphytes quickly make up for any root loss by producing new ones immediately after potting, providing that it is done at some time during the spring months. The roots therefore can be cut away using a sharp pruning knife and slicing around the inside of the basket. This enables the plant to be gently prised free from the base, and no damage is done to any part of the plant above the surface.

By the time the *Encyclia pentotis* has been removed from its existing square wooden basket, it will have little of its original root system left, and with the removal of the old compost there will be nothing to hold the plant in the new basket. Using a length of plastic-coated wire and a pair of pliers position the plant in its new elongated basket with the oldest, leafless pseudobulbs to one end, so that the front of the plant is close to the other end, with sufficient room available for at least two years' growth. The plant can now be wired firmly into position by taking a length of wire around one bottom slat and the rhizome, in between two pseudobulbs towards the back of the plant, and twisting it tight. The rhizome is hard and the wire will not cut into it. It may be necessary to put two or three wire ties to secure the plant.

The back half of the plant is now fixed by its rhizome which is resting on the bottom of the basket. The basket is now filled with compost, a little at a time starting by filling around the back half of the plant which will just cover the rhizome. With the front portion it is possible to hold the newer pseudobulbs in a slightly raised position, pouring the compost underneath and around the front growth so that when the basket is full and the bark has been pressed down the leading pseudobulbs are sitting on the surface, and only the back half of the rhizome has been covered.

An identical-shaped plant, this time *Epidendrum ciliare*, six months after having been potted into a long shallow wooden basket. The speedy recovery of the root system can clearly be seen; the new white roots have penetrated the compost, some attaching themselves to the basket and others growing downward underneath the basket, their growing tips searching out the moisture in the air. The plant has two new growths which are developing rapidly on the right.

Since being placed in the basket this plant has been carefully watered, being kept just slightly moist until the roots were seen. It was well sprayed over its leaves and pseudobulbs which helped to reduce the loss of moisture through the leaves, and in particular the surface of the compost was sprayed so as not to dislodge the bark.

This regular spraying also helps to bind the compost and allow it to settle. When normal watering is resumed it will be less likely to wash out of the basket. It may now be preferable to dip the basket in water to ensure a thorough soaking, and here again care must be taken to avoid the compost being washed away. Later, as more roots are produced they will hold the bark in place, but until then regular heavy spraying is probably best.

Once established, orchids growing in baskets will benefit from the extra light given them closer to the glass, but when newly placed in the basket they should be allowed to settle for a few weeks until hanging them up. *Epidendrum ciliare* is one example which will bloom more freely as a result.

PREPARING AN ORCHID TREE

A most attractive addition to any orchid house can be the inclusion of a natural tree branch covered with epiphytic orchids. This is not at all difficult and can be greatly satisfying to make. More or less any type of tree branch is suitable. Oak is ideal because of the rough surface and nicely twisting shapes. Apple wood is also very acceptable, and although it has a smoother bark some excellent shaped branches can be found. Less suitable are the shiny, straight branches of cherry, or any resinous pine trees. The branch should be from a live tree and the side branches cut off or trimmed back until the desired shape is formed. If a natural tree branch is difficult to acquire, a similar effect can be created using pieces of cork bark sold by florists for flower arranging. Thin tubes of cork bark can be fitted together to form an artificial tree which will look just as good when completed. A simple base is made for the tree which is then free-standing and can be moved if required. Alternatively, a permanently fixed tree can be made to fit a particular space. This can be nailed into position within the greenhouse or indoor growing case.

There is a whole variety of epiphytic orchids which can be attached to the tree. The species are more suitable than hybrids, particularly those with fine rooting systems, which will adjust in no time. Consideration should be given to plants which all require similar conditions throughout the year. Plan the plants so that the shapes complement each other, and so that they will bloom at different times.

To provide a moisture pad for the orchids, a small amount of osmunda fibre will be needed to place between the base of the plants and the bark. This will aid development of new roots at the same time supplying them with some nutrient. Osmunda fibre was for many years the standard ingredient in orchid compost. Today, although expensive, it can be purchased from some orchid nurseries. If osmunda fibre is not obtainable, sphagnum moss can be used as a substitute, or even pieces of foam rubber where neither fibre nor moss is available. The rubber will provide the necessary moisture if not nutrients. Whatever is available should be used in a damp condition. Green plastic-coated wire is ideal for tying the plants onto the tree; this will remain for many months before rusting through, by which time the plants will have anchored themselves firmly and have no need of any other support. A small pair of pliers will be handy for securing the wires around the plants, and a pair of scissors for use in the final trimming.

Once all the necessary tools are to hand, and the plants have been selected, the plants can be cleaned of all compost. Dead roots can be cut right back to the base of the plant and live roots trimmed accordingly. Live roots made within a pot will not succeed as aerial roots, but new aerial roots will grow and replace them. Should the plants have already made some aerial roots outside their pot they can be left intact.

The decision now is where to place each plant so that it contributes most to the attractiveness of the finished tree. Usually the plants seem to decide for themselves, looking just right in a particular situation. Some plants may look best on or near the main branch, whereas others will hang daintily from the extremities of a side twig. Bear in mind also that they must have space to grow. The plants should not be crowded onto the tree. Six plants would be quite enough to a tree, say, 3 ft (1 m) high.

Taking the first plant and a suitably-sized wad of damp osmunda fibre or similar material, place the latter against the tree with the plant on top. Any exposed, non-aerial roots can be tucked underneath the fibre. Once the plant's exact position has been settled, a length of the wire is taken around the branch and plant and pulled as tight as possible with the pliers, and then twisted, and the end cut off short. Two or three ties may be necessary to secure the plant, which by now must be very firm in its position. If this is done from the back of the tree, very little of the wire will show at the front. Our illustration shows a monopodial *Vanda cristata* being positioned, with the wire being placed around the lower leafless part of the rhizome. With sympodial orchids, the wire must pass between the pseudo-bulbs and never cut into them.

As the tree begins to take shape it is amazing how different some of the plants look out of their pots. Dendrobiums which may have needed several stakes to keep them upright look much more comfortable when allowed to assume a naturally pendent habit. Those plants which were already supporting aerial roots give the tree a mature look.

At this stage one or two other plants can be added if desired. These may include some of the smaller growing epiphytic tillandsias. Any of these are compatible with the orchids and will enhance the finished tree. Small epiphytic ferns can also be used, although these will grow at a faster rate than the orchids and will have to be removed if they become too large. Fast-growing plants should be avoided as these will shortly dominate the tree.

Finally trim the osmunda fibre with scissors. This is done for neatness, and will put the finishing touch to the tree. Any pieces of fibre which have become loose can be trimmed off or wired back into position.

The completed tree can now be sprayed, wetting the plants and bark alike. From now on the tree will require spraying two or three times a day during the summer, and less in winter. With little in the way of compost around the base of the plants there is no danger of overwatering, but as shrivelling from underwatering can occur quite rapidly moisture is important.

Within a few weeks aerial roots will grow and attach the plants in their own way. It should be several years before any of the plants need to be disturbed.

BARK CULTURE

Bark culture is best suited to those orchid species which produce one pseudobulb some distance above the previous one, a long upward-growing rhizome joining them. Orchids are grown in pots purely for convenience, but culture on bark is much closer to their natural mode of life. A weak or sick epiphytic species will often make a remarkable recovery when placed on a piece of bark.

Orchids growing on bark will require 'rebarking' at regular intervals, although not as often as those grown in pots. A plant can remain on one piece of bark for several years before being in need of any disturbance. If a plant outgrows its piece of bark by growing continually upward, it will not affect the plant, provided that it is given sufficient moisture by regular spraying and has plenty of aerial roots from the newest pseudobulbs. However, there inevitably comes a time when rebarking is desirable to improve the looks of a plant. This is best done in the spring, when new roots are about to start.

It is possible to use a variety of tree barks or branches, but the most popular is cork bark. This has a rough, attractive appearance, the roots can get a good grip, and it is long-lasting.

Oncidium flexuosum is an ideal species to grow on bark. This plant shows its health in the plump, shining pseudobulbs and mass of aerial roots. This is one species where roots can grow to 3 ft (1 m) long and become a thick mat. The plant which has five pseudobulbs, three in leaf, and a new growth just showing, will be left intact. The oldest bulbs are still green so need not be removed.

For rebarking a larger piece of bark will be required, plus a wad of osmunda fibre or possibly live, green sphagnum moss, a pair of pliers, a pair of scissors and a length of green plastic-coated wire. A piece of rigid wire should be inserted at one end to form a hook from which to hang the plant.

The old wire can be cut and pulled out, when it will probably be found that the plant is well rooted onto its bark. Careful teasing will lift the plant and its osmunda base clear of the bark, and the old fibre can be left in place to be used again.

Having carefully removed the plant from its bark, the dead roots or pseudobulbs can be cut away. One of the advantages of bark culture is that there is hardly any disturbance to the plant, and its entire root system can be left intact; there is no need of root trimming. Even roots slightly damaged during the rebarking operation can be left on the plant. Exposed to the air they will simply heal themselves and continue to grow.

The pad of osmunda fibre or sphagnum moss is placed the whole length on the rough side of the bark with the plant positioned directly on top of it. The oldest pseudobulbs should go to one end with maximum space left at the other end for the plant to continue its upward-growing habit. There is no danger of overbarking, as there is with overpotting, but a long slender piece of bark will suit better than a very broad piece.

The roots should be laid carefully against the fibre or moss pad and spread out where necessary. It only remains to wire the plant into position with a number of wire ties along the length of the plant, with one extra tie above the plant to hold the fibre or moss placed there in position. It is important that the plant should be held securely by the wire, and not wobble about. The rhizome between the pseudobulbs is hard, it is the hardest part of the plant, and there is little danger of snapping it by pulling the wire too tight. In our experience it is the wire which breaks if pulled too hard! The wire twists can be to the rear of the bark, out of sight.

Finally, the osmunda fibre or sphagnum moss base is neatly trimmed and any loose pieces tucked in. Where live sphagnum moss has been used, with regular after spraying, this will grow creating a lovely green natural base to the plant. It can also be used as a guide to sufficient watering. It will only grow if kept wet enough, and will turn grey when dry, a timely reminder to spray or dip!

REVERSING GROWTH

Chysis bractescens is an untidy plant to grow, and if grown upright will continually strive to turn itself the other way. Eventually the pseudobulbs grow out at all angles. Taking a closer look at this plant, it will be found that the heavy, club-shaped pseudobulbs are wasted at the base; they grow from a considerably thick, strong rhizome and swell out as they mature, consequently becoming top-heavy. Even when accommodated in an open basket this plant will look decidedly uncomfortable, and the best answer is to grow it in a pendent position on a piece of bark, or as illustrated above on a wooden raft.

The plant is removed from the basket in the usual way, and cleaned of its bark compost. The bare-rooted plant is then placed on the raft with a pad of osmunda fibre, into which the roots have been folded, between the plant and the wood.

One of the problems with growing orchids in open baskets is that not only will their roots come through the sides of the basket, but often the new growths do as well! When this happens, the result is an awkward-shaped plant with pseudobulbs in all directions. Although such a plant can be left to its own devices, sooner or later the job of repotting must be attempted, and the longer the plant has been left the harder this becomes. Our *Stanhopea wardii* has a number of pseudobulbs which are in an upright position within the basket, and two fully mature pseudobulbs which have grown at right angles outside of the pot. In order to remove the plant without harming it, it will be necessary to cut away the basket around the area where the pseudobulbs have grown. Having done this the plant is divided into three pieces, two flowering size divisions and a couple of leafless backbulbs which can be propagated from if wished.

The main part of the plant is now the piece with the leading pseudobulbs at an angle to the rest of the plant. Having divided the plant it will now be possible to pot this main piece with the leading pseudobulbs brought into an upright position and the older pseudobulbs laid on their sides and partially buried by the compost. The plant is now back to an upright position and is ready to grow on

again undisturbed for the next few years. The remaining piece of plant and the back bulbs can also be potted in the same way.

Once growing, the backbulb propagations will remain in their pots for about six months to a year, and can then be 'dropped on'. The backbulb from which they have grown can be left attached to the new growth until it eventually becomes exhausted and dies.

PROPAGATION

The propagation of orchid plants is one way of increasing the numbers in your collection, and it can be very satisfying to grow a young plant on to flowering size. Many sympodial orchids can be propagated by removal of the oldest backbulbs – those pseudobulbs which have discarded their foliage and have become surplus to the plant's requirements. Not all leafless pseudobulbs should be removed for this purpose as this may reduce the strength of the plant. Ideally the plant should be left with at least four pseudobulbs, including those in leaf, on the main plant. The excess pseudobulbs can be removed by slicing them from the plant with a sharp knife. The cut should be made downward to sever the rhizome.

The severed backbulb will grow provided that it is alive. A live backbulb is plump, or just slightly shrivelled and green. On cymbidiums the pseudobulb should be green beneath its sheaths. A pseudobulb must also have at least one live embryo growth or 'eye' at its base from which it will grow. These eyes are most easily seen on *Cymbidium* or *Cattleya* backbulbs, where they appear as a triangular-shaped swelling at the base of the bulb. These may be blackish on the surface, but will be green inside. Only if the eye is black inside and out is it dead and incapable of growth. Not all backbulbs have spare eyes.

Some sympodial orchids have a number of surplus eyes at the base, and further along the pseudobulb; usually those lower down are the strongest. The main genera which these include are cymbidiums, cattleyas, coelogynes, encyclias, and dendrobiums. Other sympodial orchids, mainly the odontoglossums and their intergeneric hybrids, are most reluctant to grow from backbulbs. Their embryo growths seem to deteriorate after a year or two, and old pseudobulbs seldom grow. For this reason these orchids are usually propagated by *front* pseudobulb division. Paphiopedilums are sympodial orchids without pseudobulbs and they can, on occasion, be propagated.

From the time of removing a backbulb from the plant, it can take about six weeks before any sign of growth movement is seen, and in some cases it can be considerably longer. Provided that the backbulb remains plump it may be left in the hope that it will eventually grow. It may even take up to a year before growth is seen. During this time the backbulb should be kept just moist; an occasional spray over the compost surface will be sufficient until the new growth is seen. Even then water must be given sparingly until the new roots are seen. Roots follow growth, and the roots take up the moisture.

Monopodial orchids can also be propagated by various means, although it is not quite so easy, and usually comes about as a result of damage to the growing centre. Otherwise, with vandas and the like, only after several years' growth is there a chance of propagating. Phalaenopsis are unique in the orchid family, and will propagate from the old flowering stems.

Natural propagation will occur with many orchids without any help from the grower. This may happen if the basal eyes have been damaged, but more often is a natural process. A number of the long-caned dendrobiums, particularly the *nobile* type, are notorious for producing 'keikis', as these propagations are known, instead of flowers which appear from the same nodes along the canes in the spring. This willingness to self-propagate becomes a matter of culture, and it is the grower who, albeit inadvertently, determines growths or flower buds.

Our illustration on the left shows two plants, *Cyrtopodium punctatum*, left, and *Thunia marshalliana*, right. Both these plants have produced an adventitious growth from the tip of the oldest cane quite naturally. Both are now small mature pseudobulbs with their own root system, ready in the spring to be removed and potted up on their own.

The orchids which propagate naturally more than any other must be the pleiones (above). These attractive little plants grow at great speed throughout the spring and summer months, shedding their single leaves in the autumn, and exhausting their pseudobulbs after two years. During their second, leafless year, numerous small propagations are produced from the top of the pseudobulbs, exactly where the leaf left the bulb. *P. formosana* produces up to six small propagations per pseudobulb whereas *P. humilus* produces a vast number of tiny, spiky bulbs densely crowded onto the crown of the pseudobulb. By the spring many of these young propagations will have fallen; the others may be taken off, and all are potted by standing them upright on the surface of a bark-filled pan.

Natural propagation of monopodial orchids is not abundant, usually occurring as a result of damage to the growing point. Occasionally propagations will be produced by vandas and allied orchids at around or near to the base of the plant from a leafless portion of the stem. These natural propagations should not be removed from the main plant until they are sufficiently mature to sustain themselves. The more pairs of leaves they have, when parted, the better, and four pairs would be the minimum. By this time they should have made an independent root system. Our illustration (right) shows a young plant of just about the right size to be removed from the adult plant. However, because of its position low down on the plant, the propagation does not interfere with the adult plant in any way, and may safely be left joined if preferred.

Artificial propagation of tall rhizomed monopodial orchids can be encouraged if a long leafless section is left at the base of the plant, and the green leafed part above carries plenty of aerial roots, and is therefore independent of the lower section. If the top portion of the plant is removed, by cutting through the rhizome below the leaves and roots, the lower portion is likely to produce a new growth. This can be further encouraged by wrapping damp moss around a section of the rhizome and covering with a square of polythene (above). Provided that the moss inside the polythene is kept moist, new growth will be encouraged underneath. About every three or four weeks the polythene can be undone and the stem inspected for signs of new growth. Once seen, the moss and polythene can be left off.

The artificial propagation of dendrobiums, by cutting a pseudobulb, also known as a cane, into short lengths, is a less haphazard way of ensuring that one's stock of a particular plant is increased. This method can be applied only to those species or hybrids which produce flowers the whole length of their canes rather than from the top nodes only. These include *Dendrobium nobile*, shown here, *D. aureum, D. wardianum, D. transparens*, and *D. superbum*.

A leafless cane should be selected which has not flowered and which will not weaken the plant when removed. Our illustration shows a plant with three older, flowered canes on the left, one cane in leaf and a surplus cane on the right. This cane will produce flowers in the next season if left on the plant. The grower must therefore be prepared to forego flowers for one season in order to gain a number of propagations from this cane. Older, flowered canes will have used up their embryo eyes and will no longer be capable of further growth. Old, unflowered canes which are badly shrivelled will be unlikely to grow, as also any canes which have turned brown or soft.

The cane which has been selected for removal should be cut off at the base. The ideal time to do this is late winter, or early spring, before the embryo buds have started to show any activity.

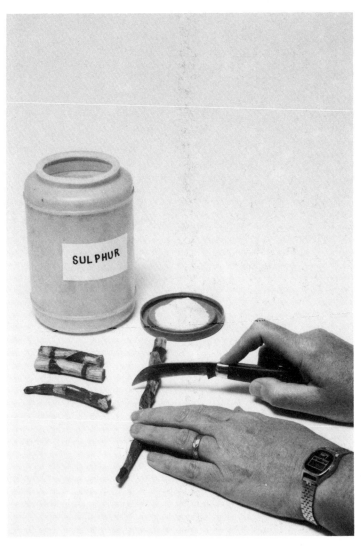

The cane is now cut into short lengths with a sharp knife, cutting in between the swollen ridges along the cane where the leaves were attached. Each ridge contains a 'node' or small swelling directly opposite from which a new growth will come. The severed ends are then dipped into sulphur or charcoal powder to seal and dry the area to prevent any rotting.

From here there are two methods which can be followed. The chopped pieces of cane can be inserted at intervals around the edge of a community pot, or half pot. Place each piece in an upright position and push into the compost until the 'node' is level with the surface of the compost. Keep slightly moist until new growth is seen. Not all the pieces may grow; those from the top of the cane are more likely to show signs of growth than those from the bottom. Those pieces which do grow will do so fairly soon after potting, and by six to ten weeks leaves and roots should be apparent. At this stage examine the remaining pieces of cane for signs of growth. After a little more time, if they have still not grown, these can be thrown away, as also any pieces which have turned brown or become soft. Be particularly wary of small slugs and snails at this stage. The young succulent growths can disappear overnight.

The second method entails placing the pieces of cane in a small seedling tray which has been prepared for them with a fine grade of bark filled to half-way. They can be either laid flat in the tray as illustrated or plunged upright into the bark to half of their length. Just sufficient space should be left between them for the new growth. If covered with a sheet of clear food wrapping the moisture will be kept inside the tray and speed growth. A piece of glass or taut polythene will do as well. In this way it is easy to keep an eye on the propagations and remove any weeds that may also find these ideal growing conditions. An alternative potting material, which has proved highly successful in encouraging roots, is sphagnum moss. This is a bog plant with feathery stems which when growing wild behaves like a sponge, and the water can literally be wrung from it. It also contains iodine, and orchids will grow very well in it for a limited time. Only fresh, green sphagnum moss should be used, and this will continue to grow when used in this way. From time to time it will be necessary to trim the moss to prevent it from swamping the slower growing propagations. As soon as the new leaf tips touch the protective covering it can be removed.

The propagations can remain in their tray for up to a year, by which time they will be smart young plants with their first completed pseudobulb and a strong new growth indicating a much larger second pseudobulb. At this stage bottom heat can be a great advantage to the young growing plants, and this can be provided by putting the pot or tray inside a propagator with a soil warming unit. The extra warmth will help the young plants to develop faster, but also cause them to dry out quicker, so particular attention should be paid to watering. Warm, dry conditions can cause an early death as easily as cold and damp. This bottom heat is a temporary aid to the young developing plants, and should not be used permanently, which would cause a lush, soft growth. Also at this young stage feeding should be very light; later, as the plants build up their strength in their pseudobulbs, feeding can gradually be increased. From the time that the one-year-old plant is separated it will be another two to three years before flowering can be expected. Up to that time the young plant may or may not shed all its leaves in the winter. Whether or not this naturally occurs, some moisture should be allowed for fear of completely drying up the little plant, to such an extent that it fails to grow again the following spring.

The young plant will be complete with its own root system and quite independent of the original piece of cane from which it grew. This piece of cane will by now be withered, and can easily be separated from the young plant. When removed from its tray, the plant is now potted on into a very small pot. Take care not to pot too deeply, but 'sit' the plant on the surface, bearing in mind that the new growth must come from the base.

Here we illustrate (opposite) the natural method of propagation which has occurred on a similar plant of *Dendrobium nobile*. Unfortunately, these strong young propagations are not always as welcome as they should be; they have grown in place of flowers and are a direct result of the cultural conditions under which the plant has been growing. In their natural environment dendrobiums are subjected to extremes of climate which are necessary for the development of flowers.

Under cultivation there should be the greatest possible variation between the summer and winter conditions. High summer temperatures with an abundance of moisture should be offset by much cooler, very dry and light winters. If propagations are to be encouraged, warmer winters with less resting will make the difference between flowers and growths.

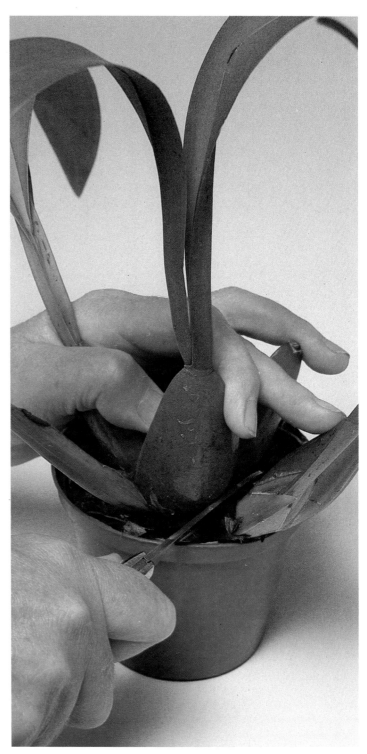

The propagation of *Odontoglossum* and related hybrids can be achieved by removing the *front* pseudobulb. This group of orchids very seldom produce more than one growth each year and the older pseudobulbs seem to lose the ability to grow from dormant eyes within a year or two. Because of the drastic action required it is not advisable to take front bulb propagations unless an extra plant is most definitely required. There is more risk to the plant than when removing the older backbulbs. The removal of the leading pseudobulb should not be attempted on a plant with less than four pseudobulbs.

The leading pseudobulb should be severed, preferably in the spring when the new growth can just be seen. The plant is then left in its pot, without further disturbance until a new growth is sighted on the pseudobulb immediately behind the severed leading pseudobulb. This may take a few weeks, but when it shows the plant is ready for repotting at the earliest opportunity, probably in late summer. This process avoids disturbing the two divisions of the plant at a time when the root system alone must sustain the front division, and less shrivelling to the leading pseudobulb will occur.

The two portions may be repotted separately. The single pseudobulb will require a small pot until it gains in size. It may also require support to keep it firm in the pot until a new root system has formed.

Having achieved two plants from one, it will probably be a year or two before either portion blooms. If an attempt is made by the new growth on the single pseudobulb to bloom, it will considerably help the plant if this is removed.

Such division of odontoglossums and related hybrids should not be undertaken too frequently to disturb the health and vigour of the plant.

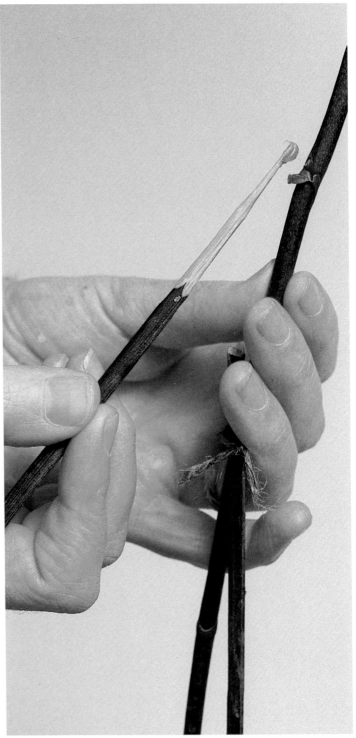

The propagation of phalaenopsis can be carried out in a unique way. This is by flower stem propagation and on certain species occurs frequently by natural process. The hybrids are less inclined to propagate of their own accord. On a flowering stem it will be noticed that there are a number of nodes at intervals along the length of stem below the buds. The nodes carry the dormant eyes, which can develop into further buds or leaves. When the flowers have passed their prime, cut the flower spike below the buds midway to the first node, and apply 'keiki' or hormone paste to the node.

If the cut flower stem is left undisturbed, it will more than likely develop further buds and give yet another spray of flowers. This is a perfectly normal way of achieving more flowers and extending the flowering time of a particular plant. However, this should only be done if the plant is strong enough, and growing a new leaf at the time. If the continual flowering is at the expense of a new leaf forming, or, if the quality and size of the flowers being produced is decreasing, the whole stem should be removed and the plant given time to recover before flowering again.

Where a new plant is required from the stem 'keiki' or hormone paste will have been applied to the node. Keiki is the name for the new plant grown from stem propagation, and keiki paste is a hormone compound especially produced for this purpose. Where the keiki paste has been used, it will with luck alter the cells to create a new plant instead of flowers. It must be stated, however, that this is not always successful, and works better on some phalaenopsis than others. Much depends upon the breeding of the plant. Nevertheless, it is worth a try to increase one's plants.

If all has been successfully achieved, the result after approximately three to six months will be a fine little plant with two to three leaves and its own aerial roots. The keiki is then ready to be removed from its stem and potted up on its own. However, if this is in the middle of winter, delay potting until the spring. To avoid any damage to the keiki the old flower stem should be cut about an inch or two from the keiki. When potting, the stem can be used to hold the plant firmly in its pot, using small wire loops to secure.

Phalaenopsis grow rapidly from young plants, and our six-month-old keiki will be capable of producing flowers in another eighteen months. As the plant grows steadily it should be repotted carefully, without disturbance to the brittle roots, on an annual basis. Growing such a plant on to flowering is one of the greatest thrills an orchid grower can experience, and there is no finer-looking plant than a *Phalaenopsis* in full shining growth.

HYBRIDISATION

In the nursery of James Veitch & Son in Exeter, Devon, in about 1850, there was an orchid grower whose job it was to cultivate the vast number of species that the company had been importing for many years. His name was John Dominy, and he was to become famous as the first man successfully to hybridise and flower orchid plants from seed. Following the suggestion of a local surgeon and amateur botanist, John Harris, the first tentative steps were made, and in 1853 several orchids were crossed with each other. It is probable that the first orchids to be raised were cattleyas but these took many years before they bloomed. The hybrid, *Calanthe* Dominyii (*C. furcata* × *C. masuca*), made about the same time, was the first to bloom in 1856. Since then a wave of hybridising has continued to this day and is increasing every year. In a never-ending search for new shapes and colours, man-made varieties are constantly being bred. The ultimate aim of most gardeners is to produce a new variety and the hybridising of orchids is something that every orchid grower can try. When choosing two flowers they will be more compatible if from the same or closely-related genera, and if the species come from the similar countries of origin or habitats. The colour of the flowers, numbers on a stem, and the quality, all can be considered.

By looking through the Sanders List of Orchid Hybrids you can find out whether the cross you have in mind has been made before. Having made your cross, it can take up to twelve months for ripe seed to be produced.

This is followed by a growing period of perhaps five to six years before your first flowers are likely to be seen. This long term should not put off the enthusiastic hybridiser. The pleasure of raising your own orchids from seed is well worth the effort and patience. Memories are short, therefore a careful record should be kept from the time of making the cross. Start your own stud book by numbering your cross with a record of which plant carried the capsule and which gave the pollen, along with the date of pollination and any other information you want to record such as whether the pollination was successful the first time or if subsequent crossings had to take place.

Although the number of hybrids runs into many thousands there is still much to be achieved, and in our opinion the surface has only been scratched. Many new lines of breeding remain to be started and the future of hybridising is one of the most exciting fields in which to become involved.

Orchids are different from other plants in that grains of pollen are formed into masses called pollinia. These vary in number, but two or four are most common in cultivated orchids. Most are insect-pollinated, which helps to explain their evolution which has resulted in the almost unlimited range of size and shape of blooms to attract the insects. In spite of this great variation all orchid flowers conform to the same basic pattern and are all pollinated in the same way. The male and female reproductive parts are fused into one organ, the column, with the pollinia carried at the end and protected by the anther cap. Just below the anther is a stigmatic surface area to which pollen is transferred during pollination.

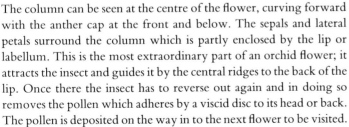

The column can be seen at the centre of the flower, curving forward with the anther cap at the front and below. The sepals and lateral petals surround the column which is partly enclosed by the lip or labellum. This is the most extraordinary part of an orchid flower; it attracts the insect and guides it by the central ridges to the back of the lip. Once there the insect has to reverse out again and in doing so removes the pollen which adheres by a viscid disc to its head or back. The pollen is deposited on the way in to the next flower to be visited.

When pollinating, be sure that the flower you have chosen is fresh. Here a bloom has been tilted back to show the anther cap which is easily removed to reveal the two golden yellow sacs attached by threads to the stigmatic patch. Behind this is the stigma situated in a small hollow.

A cocktail stick is ideal to lift the stigmatic patch which holds the pollen. You will find this comes away freely. If the pollen is not a good colour, or is blackened, the flower may be too old.

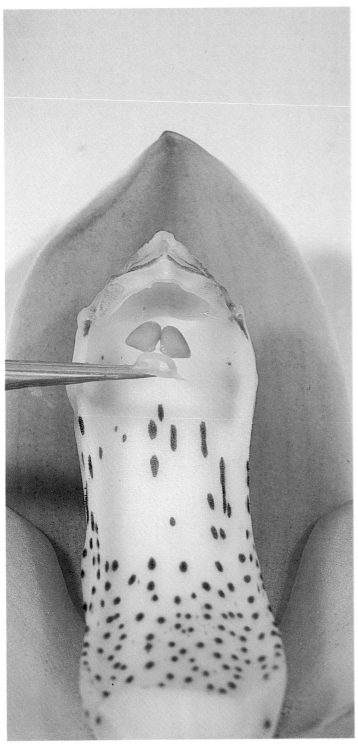

After removing the anther cap and pollen from the flower that is to bear the capsule it is ready to receive the pollen from your second flower. Carefully convey the new pollen attached by the stigmatic patch to the cocktail stick to the stigmatic surface which will be found just below the pollen. The new pollen will fit easily into the space and adhere to the sticky surface. The thousands of grains contained in each pollen mass will soon start to grow in the sticky bed, each grain sending a microscopic thread through the passageways of the column.

As the stick is removed upwards and away from the stigma the pollen mass remains firmly attached to the sticky bed with the stigmatic patch adhering to the stick. Two long threads of elastic-like material will, at first, extend before snapping. The pollination of the flower is now complete. When there is a great difference of size between the two flowers being crossed, pollen is taken from the small flower and placed onto the larger bloom using two to three sets of the smaller pollen to ensure fertility.

Within a few days if pollination has been successful the end of the column will swell to enclose the pollen masses. On cymbidiums the lip will turn bright red and the sepals and petals lose their colour and wilt. On *Phalaenopsis* flowers the sepals and petals thicken and turn green as they become full of chlorophyll. Any flower on a spray can be pollinated, but it is usually one of the lower flowers which is selected. One seed capsule, or on very strong plants two or three, is as much as any plant should be asked to carry in one year.

The stem immediately behind the flower will gradually develop as the fertilisation of seeds takes place. A *Cymbidium* capsule will swell to the size of a lemon and other orchids can produce even larger capsules. These capsules, often incorrectly referred to as seed 'pods', may contain many thousands of minute seeds. A record attached to the capsule shows the date of pollination and the parents used. The unpollinated flowers can be removed from the main stem, which should be left intact above the developing capsule. It will remain green and ensure a good sap supply to the capsule.

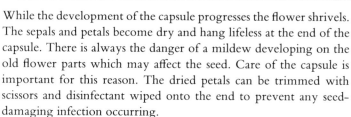

While the development of the capsule progresses the flower shrivels. The sepals and petals become dry and hang lifeless at the end of the capsule. There is always the danger of a mildew developing on the old flower parts which may affect the seed. Care of the capsule is important for this reason. The dried petals can be trimmed with scissors and disinfectant wiped onto the end to prevent any seed-damaging infection occurring.

The extra strain caused to a valuable mother plant is the reason for seldom pollinating more than the first or second bloom on a long spike.

A seed capsule should be harvested before it splits and the seed is contaminated or lost. As the capsule ripens, usually indicated by a slight yellowing along the seams, it will start to split, releasing the minute seed which drifts down on any movement of air. Watch for the signs when a capsule looks ripe, which may be any time after six months on the plant and remove it before it splits.

It sometimes happens that insects pollinate flowers. The resulting seed capsules should be discarded as crosses made by unknown parents are not worth the years of waiting needed to flower them.

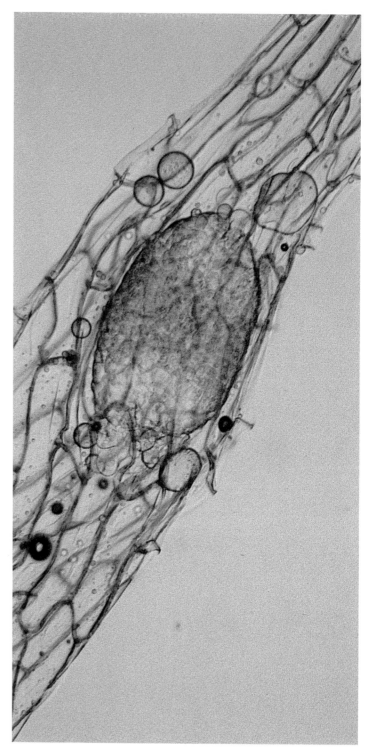

Not all capsules will carry seed; even the fattest capsules can be found to be empty. Similarly, not all seeds are fertile. Because they are so minute, it is impossible to identify the fertility of individual seeds without the aid of a microscope. A small powered, 75 to 100 magnification, student's microscope is ideal for this purpose. A sprinkling of seeds on a slide will quickly reveal whether they are fertile. Soaking a few seeds in a solution of sugar water for twenty-four hours will make them swell, and this will make it easier to study them under the microscope.

Although ripe and ready to leave the capsule, the orchid seed is nevertheless very immature. It consists of merely a single cell held in an open network of a husk. Preparation to sow should be made at once, as fertility quickly drops once the seed is isolated from the capsule although it is possible to store orchid seed for short periods under dry and refrigerated conditions.

Orchid seed is carried in thermals to very high altitudes where it can remain suspended in deep freeze until it gradually drifts back to earth to germinate.

Paphiopedilums and related genera are the only orchids in cultivation which require a different pollination to that previously described. These orchids carry their pollinia in two solid masses, one each side of the central column or staminode. One of these can be removed carefully on the point of a cocktail stick as shown. An insect would crawl through the back of the pouch and pollinate the flower out of sight.

To reach the pollinia on a *Paphiopedilum* flower, it is necessary either to remove the pouch altogether or, if you do not wish to spoil the appearance of the bloom, cut a small square hole with a razor blade at the top in the back of the pouch. This will give access to the stigmatic surface where the pollen is to be placed. This is carried out more easily if the pot is laid on its side, which makes a more convenient angle at which to examine the flower.

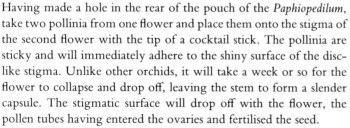

Having made a hole in the rear of the pouch of the *Paphiopedilum*, take two pollinia from one flower and place them onto the stigma of the second flower with the tip of a cocktail stick. The pollinia are sticky and will immediately adhere to the shiny surface of the disc-like stigma. Unlike other orchids, it will take a week or so for the flower to collapse and drop off, leaving the stem to form a slender capsule. The stigmatic surface will drop off with the flower, the pollen tubes having entered the ovaries and fertilised the seed.

The seed capsules of paphiopedilums do not swell to the same size as other orchids and at first little difference is noticed to the remaining stem. After the flower has fallen the capsule should remain green and healthy. Should it dry up and wither, pollination has not taken place. Paphiopedilums do not yield enormous quantities of seed and some hybrids may only produce a few dozens of fertile seeds. The upright capsule can remain for nine to twelve months on the plant before ripening and showing signs of splitting.

In its natural state the orchid seed germinates and grows only in conjunction with a microscopic fungus which releases to the seed all the necessary nutrients and trace elements for its development and growth. By replacing these chemicals artificially and suspending them in a jelly, the need for the fungal mycelium is thus bypassed. Most orchid seed will germinate on a general formula, but for certain groups more specialised formulae are necessary. When purchasing a ready-prepared medium, which is available from specialist firms, you can check that you are getting the correct medium for your seed.

In their natural state very few of the thousands of seeds produced by one capsule will germinate. Under artificial conditions, where techniques similar to those used in the laboratory are employed, we can successfully raise 100 per cent of the seed which is sown. Today, you can purchase ready-to-use sowing kits. You have only to follow the instructions on the bottle and pour the ingredients into a litre or two of distilled water to produce a nutritious and sterile medium on which to germinate your seed. After boiling for about twenty minutes the ingredients will be thoroughly dissolved. The liquid is then measured into conical flasks or similar containers which can be sterilised and tightly stoppered. The flasks must be sterilised, and the easiest method is to put them in a pressure cooker for approximately twenty minutes. When you remove the flasks place them on racks, on their sides, and allow the jelly a day to cool and set.

All the materials mentioned can be purchased in small quantities by firms specialising in the needs of orchid growers, and the work can be easily achieved in a kitchen.

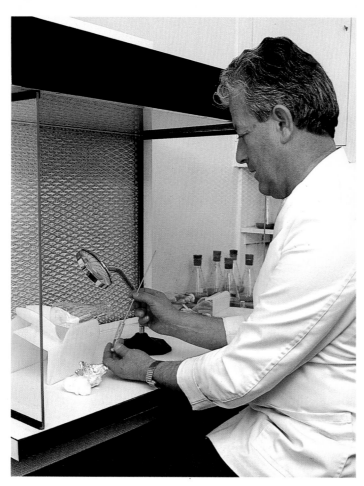

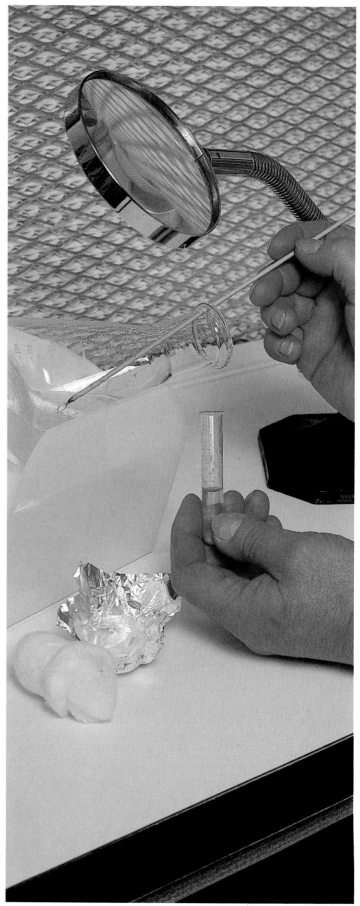

The orchid seed, which is sterile within the capsule, quickly becomes contaminated by microscopic fungus spores immediately it is exposed to the air. Inside the flasks the fungus spores will grow with alarming speed, destroying the seed within hours. Therefore the seed needs to be sterilised before being introduced to the sterile flasks. With the sowing kits, which can be purchased from firms that specialise in orchid sundries, comes the appropriate chemical. This is designed to kill the fungus spores but leave the seed unharmed. The sterilising chemical is prepared in a flask, the seed straight from the capsule added and shaken thoroughly for ten minutes. Then comes the most difficult part of the operation which is to introduce the sterilised seed to the surface of the jelly without incurring contamination. Some loss can be introduced at this stage. Where expensive sterilising equipment is lacking, equal success can be achieved by working at the cooker over a bowl of boiling water which is creating a sterile area. Thoroughly wash your hands and all equipment before starting, then remove the seed from the sterilant with a thin wire loop purchased with the sowing kit. By this means, a minimum amount of sterilant and a maximum amount of seed is transferred at a time. After uncorking the flask in the sterile area, carefully spread the seed on the surface of the jelly. You can easily over-sow, and this can be disastrous when the young seedlings grow, so a thin layer is essential. While keeping the flask in the sterile area, re-stopper as tightly as possible before repeating with the next flask. Place flasks in a well shaded area.

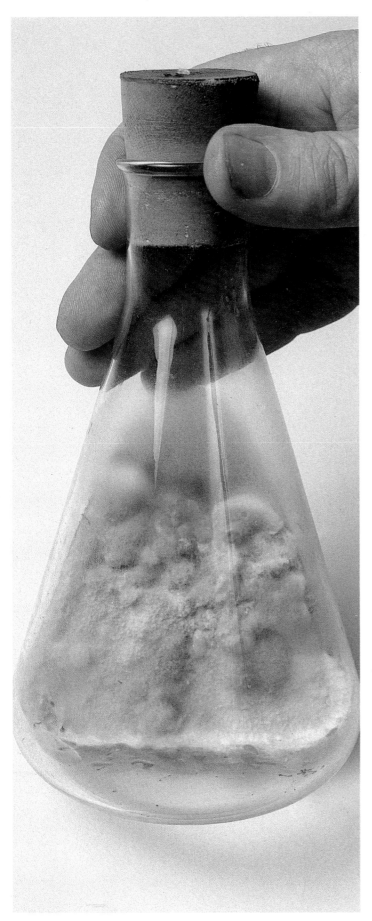

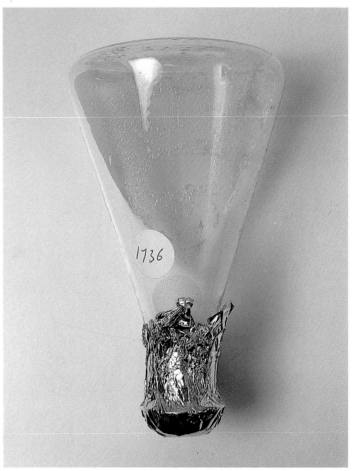

Within a few days of sowing your seed in the specially prepared sterile containers, you will know whether you have been initially successful in keeping out all moulds. This will be so, provided that the flasks have been tightly re-stoppered to ensure maintained sterility inside the flask. The stopper can be either a solid rubber bung with a small hole filled with cotton wool, or a bung made completely of cotton wool and covered with silver foil. The cotton wool will allow a small amount of filtered air to penetrate the flask as it expands and contracts with the rise and fall of the temperature. Obviously some air is essential. From now on keep the flasks in a high temperature of 60–65° F (16–18° C). Within a few weeks you will see tiny specks of green appearing as the seeds start to produce their own chlorophyll (above). At this stage they are too small to produce leaves and roots immediately, and develop first into protocorms. The protocorms build up sufficient food to sustain further development which will follow within weeks or months of this stage. Unsuccessful flasks which have become contaminated by fungus spores (left) must be discarded immediately they are seen. The moulds grow rapidly on the surface of the jelly and could spread into other flasks. Most orchids produce vast quantities of seed, and it is only a small fraction which is able to be used. If you sow one or two more flasks than required, you are allowing for the odd contamination, with more than enough left over.

When the seed-sowing has been successful and germination has occurred, the surface of the jelly where the seed was sown within the sterilised container becomes covered with a mass of miniature green spheres. Each one is a protocorm of green chlorophyll representing the orchids of the future. At this stage you can remove the protocorms to further flasks containing a stronger growing medium which have already been prepared as previously described. The flask is unstoppered and the young protocorms removed under sterile conditions and placed in a sterile dish. Any that have become stuck together can be carefully separated and any that do not look healthy can be discarded. From these mother flasks which may contain thousands of green protocorms, about 25–30 will be resown on the surface of the jelly in new flasks. At this stage of reflasking retain more than you require to allow for loss through contamination. A few of the mother flasks may be kept until the reflasked seedlings are growing successfully in case something goes wrong. It is better to overproduce at this stage and discard later to achieve the required quantity.

Our illustration above shows commercially-sown seedlings using 500cc conical flasks. Much smaller containers can be used for smaller quantities of seedlings, down to test tubes carrying a single seedling. A few seedlings in several small containers are of course safer than all your seedlings in one large container.

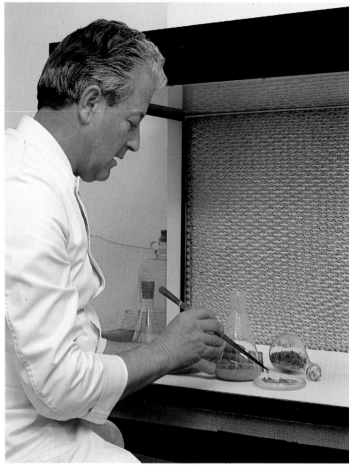

If all has gone well so far with the sowing procedure, the surface of the jelly is covered with mounds of bright green protocorms. The protocorms have grown from the seed and are the first stage of the orchid's development before leaves and roots start to grow. These protocorms now require more room to develop and at this stage are replanted into new containers, prepared beforehand, as previously described. Each protocorm is placed individually on the surface of the new sterile flasks. You can now use upright flasks to allow the growing plants more headroom. As the young plants produce a leaf from the top and a root from the bottom of the small protocorm, they begin to resemble real miniature orchids. The roots penetrate the jelly where they can take up the food and nutrients waiting for them in carefully balanced amounts. The leaves will continue to photosynthesise with the chlorophyll that is in them. On the surface of the roots will form a minute structure of fine hairs known as hypha. This should not be confused with the contamination seen earlier; it is a natural part of the plant's development. The young plants will not be disturbed again until the spring.

All sowing and reflasking in a professional laboratory is done in a special sowing cabinet. This produces a constant stream of sterile air flowing towards the operator. Providing that the tools being used are washed and swabbed with a sterilant, the risk of contamination is reduced to a minimum. In non-commercial establishments a sterile area can be created by using a bowl of steaming hot water over the cooker.

The young orchid plants remain in the flasks until they are as large and strong as possible but before they run short of nutrients. The best results are obtained by the commercial grower with a growing room rather than a greenhouse. Here, the young plants are grown under completely artificial conditions. The light is evenly controlled to the same daily amount throughout the year. The temperature is allowed to rise and fall only by the amount required for the particular orchids being grown. The minimum amount of air movement ensures that there is little contamination. In a growing room it is possible to grow a large number of flasks in a small area by shelving them in batteries.

These commercial 'battery houses' of orchids may contain meristems or seedlings. More often today the vast majority of the flasks contain meristems of the world's finest orchids. These would be the very best of their type, many awarded clones given due recognition of their outstanding qualities. Thus it is that the amateur grower can be offered first-rate, top-quality plants at no higher a price than would be paid for unflowered, and therefore unproven, seedlings.

From a single capsule will come thousands of possible plants. Of those to bloom eventually, no two will be exactly alike. Each will be an individual clone, slightly different from the rest. This is the choice open to the amateur grower: to purchase a top-quality, possibly an awarded, clone, which will bloom true to expectations and catalogue descriptions; or to take a chance by purchasing unflowered seedlings, with only the size, shape and colours of the parents as a guide to what may be expected of the progeny. Both are exciting prospects: to acquire either a really super plant, which has received world acclaim, or the unknown seedling, which could bring you an award.

Sometime during spring, within nine to twelve months from the initial sowing of the seed, the seedlings reach a stage where the roots have absorbed most of the nutrients in the jelly, and their leaves have reached the top of the flask. This is the time to remove the seedlings before more growth causes overcrowding and eventual yellowing of the seedlings. The flasks can now be handled on the open bench without the need for sterile air. The flask is unstoppered and a little water at room temperature is poured into the flask to ease the extraction of the plants, which are carefully removed using a wire hook. Each plant is drawn out through the neck and placed in a bowl of water also at room temperature. If the plants cannot be separated it is easier to break the glass rather than risk damaging the plants. This will do no harm to the seedlings which can be picked up *en bloc* and placed in a saucer of clean water. Here the plants can be separated and washed clean of all agar. Commercially-raised seedling flasks are kept in a specially-designed growing room. Here the air is maintained at an even temperature and the flasks are placed on shelves under artificial lights which are switched on automatically to give the plants the right amount of daylight in every twenty-four hours. With minimum disturbance of the atmosphere the chance of contamination is very small and the plants grow extremely well under these conditions. At this stage they will do better in this environment than if grown in a greenhouse. For the amateur a propagator placed in the greenhouse will serve just as well.

When all the plants are safely out of their container and washed of all agar they can be sorted and laid on sheets of paper to dry. If grown well they will have produced an equal amount of leaves and roots, and the protocorm from which they grow will still be visible at the base. Any particularly long roots, and also damaged roots, can be trimmed, which is preferable to winding them into the compost and breaking them.

From the contents of one container it becomes apparent that some seedlings have grown faster than others, as occurs naturally whenever you sow a packet of seeds. Some are more vigorous and will outgrow the weaker plants. Because the orchid produces an enormous quantity of seed, the practice is always to oversow. At this stage you can discard the small protocorms which have failed to produce plants and any weak seedlings which are not up to a minimum standard. Retain only the strongest plants to grow on, as there lie ahead many years of culture and the strongest stand the best chance of growing.

Seedling trays are prepared in the same way as for all young plants, a finer mixture of compost than that used for adult plants. Each seedling is carefully lowered into a small trench made with the fine point of a plant label, and firmed down with the finger and thumb. Community pots may be used if there are only a few seedlings. The plants should be well spaced to allow room for growth and inspected every day. Very soon new roots will be seen. These will be the familiar thick, white type. Remove any damped-off plants and any dead leaves at once to avoid infection. After twelve months the plants will have grown large enough to be transferred into individual pots. The leaders of phalaenopsis may be expected to bloom in about three years, whereas cattleyas and some *Cymbidium* crosses may take five or six years to reach flowering. Water these seedling trays in their early stages with great care. The finest of roses will ensure that the trays are never saturated. Neither should they become dry for any period of time. Trays that are kept evenly moist will produce the best results. When the plants have become established a programme of fertilising may be commenced depending on the time of year. With the summer ahead of them these young seedlings will grow quickly, and as soon as they have made their own root system watering will not be as critical as in the first few weeks.

Orchids produce vast quantities of seed; several hundred thousand can be expected from a single capsule. Imagine a plant bearing many flower spikes with a hundred blooms. If every one were pollinated, the capsules could produce umpteen millions of seeds. If every seed germinated the amount of orchids in the wild would be colossal, but as always in nature the production of seeds is extravagant to allow for severe loss. Just enough survive to ensure the perpetuation of the species. The extremely fine seed is carried from the mother plant on the wind and drifts many miles before it settles. It can only germinate if it comes into contact with a certain microscopic fungus, peculiar to each orchid. The fungus releases the nutrients so vital to the germination and growth of the young plant. It is these nutrients which are reproduced artificially to grow seeds in the laboratory.

If no facilities exist and you do not wish to try the artificial method already described, why not try sowing the seed by the natural method. When the early hybridisers started breeding orchids half-way through the last century, they soon discovered that the seed germinated best if sown in the same pot as the plant from which the seed came. It was not until the early part of this century that the experts learnt to cultivate the microscopic fungus so vital to germination. They grew the fungus first on a jelly similar to the method described previously and infected the seed with the fungus. Later this idea was replaced completely with chemical formulae which produced the same result. For natural sowing, harvest the capsule just before it is ready to burst, when splits begin to appear,

and check the seed for fertility as previously described using a small microscope. Some time previously you will have chosen your 'foster' plant or plants. This plant should be of the same species or genus as the seed-bearing mother plant. The foster plant must be in good health and free from any pests and diseases. It should not be in need of repotting for at least another two years, its compost fresh throughout containing live healthy roots. The surface should be as flat and even as possible. It is on this stock that you are planning to germinate your seed. Carefully remove then open the capsule and sprinkle some seed over the surface of the compost and around the base of your foster plant. If you are lucky, a few seeds will germinate, but even these few will be sufficient to meet the needs of most amateurs. Any surplus seed remaining from flask sowing can be sprinkled over a plant in this way. Our illustration shows a *Maxillaria*, an early orchid to be raised by this method. The partly ripened capsule has already split open naturally and is being held with one hand, gently tapped with the finger. This helps to spread the seed evenly over the compost.

Do not forget to label each foster plant carefully with the names of the seed sown, the date and any other information required. In days gone by hybridisers would set aside a whole bench full of plants to be used for this method, and they proved that some orchids were better host plants than others (particularly in the case of paphiopedilums which can be so successful that they are still used today as mother plants by many hybridisers).

When sowing seed the natural way, there is very little after care, apart from ensuring that the seeds do not become overtaken by mosses or ferns which can cover the surface of the foster plant.

Special care is needed, however, when watering to prevent the minute seeds from washing over the rim of the pot. Many of the seeds will be washed down, where they will lodge safely, and with luck grow.

Under the circumstances, the best and safest method of watering the foster plant is to stand the plant in a bowl of water with the surface of the compost just above the water. The moisture will soak up through the compost and prevent overwetting of the surface. Keep your foster plant watered by this method at least once a week for the next year or so. The germination of the seed can be very uneven compared with flask culture and the first sighting of seedlings does not mean that these are all that may be expected. More seedlings may appear several months later and continue to appear for any time up to a year.

It is important to stress that orchid seed must be sown fresh, and should be taken directly from the capsule to be sown. The seed deteriorates rapidly once it has left the seed capsule. For this reason packets of orchid seed offered for sale will be impossible to germinate.

Having discussed the watering of a foster plant to protect the seed from being washed away, it may still prove difficult to keep the surface constantly at an even moisture. Sprinkling the surface of the compost with a fine syringe may be the answer. This will ensure that the seed itself is kept moist, and it can be done as often as possible without harm. Amongst the rough particles of the bark the seed will gradually move down through the surface compost, although not too deep to be lost completely. The germination of the seed will be additionally helped by the foster plant being kept a little warmer than usual, but at the same time kept out of direct sunlight, especially during the summer months. Extra attention to these little details will help to keep the compost moist and the temperature even. Fertiliser is better not added to the water used on foster plants as this may prove too strong for the young seedlings and could burn any protocorms as they develop. It is better to use clean rainwater, or tap water at greenhouse temperature. If sphagnum moss is available and can be included in the compost of the foster plant it will greatly help the progress of the seedlings. Sphagnum moss is a material which in recent years has fallen out of favour with orchid growers, but in the past it was widely used with great success. Where it is used it should not be allowed to grow to such an extent that it swamps any seedlings.

Be extremely vigilant to keep slugs and snails at bay. Just one small pest such as this can eat through a year's work in a single night.

The orchid seed sown on a 'foster' plant by using the natural method will germinate in exactly the same way as those sown artificially in the flasks. The seeds which may be hidden from sight, having been washed a little way into the compost, will gradually develop into protocorms, although not always producing as much chlorophyll if they are out of the light. After a few months it will be possible to see the first signs of leaves – small green shoots – appearing on the surface. Wait until they have grown strong enough to be carefully removed. This may take another twelve months, by which time the seedlings will have leaves and roots, and will stand an inch or two (2.5–5 cm) high. To remove the seedlings without damaging the roots it may be necessary to take the foster plant out of its pot and remove the compost. These seedlings can be left with the mother plant until they have reached one pseudobulb and growth stage if you wish.

Do not disturb the young seedlings until the spring, when they have the summer growing season in front of them. They should be large enough to pot up singly in 2-in (5-cm) pots. From this stage they can be repotted annually for a couple of years, and then biennially.

Paphiopedilums are possibly the best orchids to germinate by the natural method, and until quite recent years the commercial orchid growers preferred to raise them this way. They were difficult to germinate in flasks and it took many years of research to find the ideal formulae on which to sow the seeds. Today these formulae have been perfected and paphiopedilums are almost as easy to raise as other orchids. Amateurs will still get a great deal of pleasure and satisfaction from sowing seeds on 'foster' plants. In the past the old nursery establishments kept greenhouses full of foster plants for the sole purpose of raising orchids by this method, and many thousands of seedlings were grown in this way. It is perhaps unfortunate that this skill has died out and is no longer practised today in large quantities.

Looking after a number of foster plants with seedlings can be a full-time job, but nevertheless extremely satisfying, even if only occasionally successful.

TISSUE CULTURE

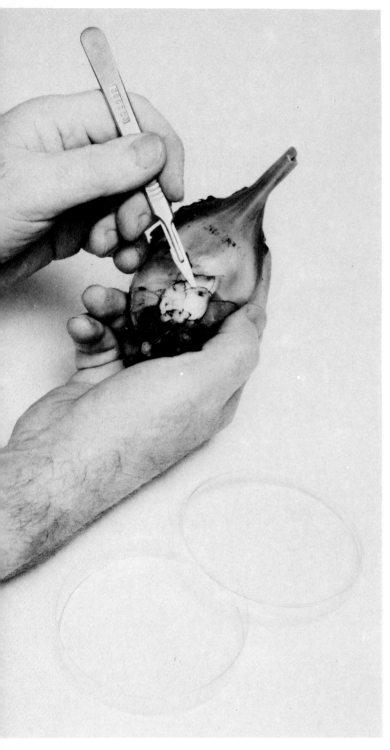

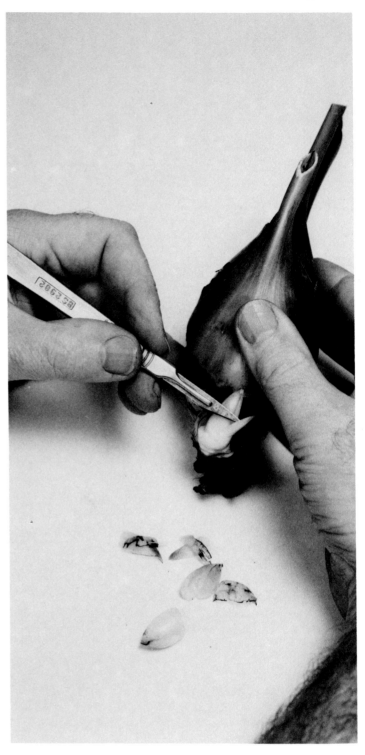

Conventional propagation by means of division and the taking of cuttings has achieved the slow increase of plants ever since they were first cultivated. It takes many years to build up a stock of a few dozen plants from propagations bearing in mind that it has already taken five or six years for the donor plants to reach maturity from seed. Propagation is slow and restricted. Seed production, although admirable, does not provide genetically-identical plants, and each generation of seed-raised plants is slightly different from the one before. Certainly when raising hybrids we are hoping for very different and improved progeny. In the past perfect specimens of

which we would like large stocks in preference to further hybridising could only be propagated by the division of one backbulb at a time. Fortunately, today, there is another method, discovered only in the last decade – propagation by tissue culture. This is usually beyond the realms of the average amateur grower, who anyway does not want to raise large quantities of a single clone. To the commercial grower, who requires thousands of identical blooms to be produced for a particular occasion, the advantages are enormous. The process of tissue culture starts by carefully dissecting the young growth, in this case on a *Cymbidium* pseudobulb which has been taken from a mature

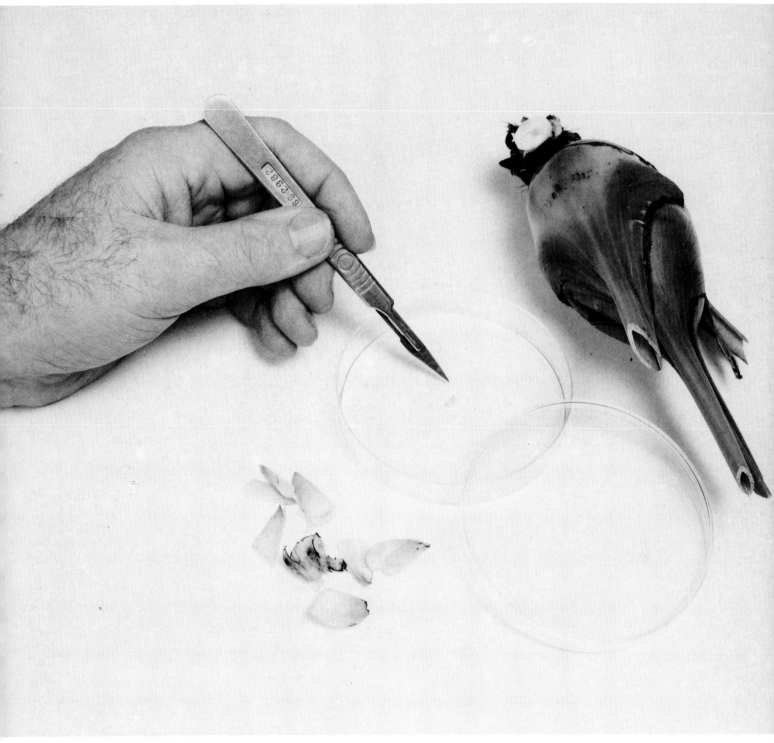

plant, until the central cell structure, known as the meristem tip, is reached. This is not unlike a protocorm in appearance. This is carefully removed and cultivated in flasks in the same way as seedlings.

This meristem will quickly produce a large green protocorm. This is then divided many times as it grows, thus increasing the stock to unlimited amounts. Many thousands of times this may be divided and cultivated on a jelly medium until the required number of plantlets is reached. These young plants in turn will take several years to reach maturity when a large stock of uniform orchids is guaranteed. This work is still in an evolutionary stage and new techniques are constantly being introduced as well as new varieties meristemmed. In theory all plants can be reproduced in this way but in practice there are some which do not increase at the rate expected of them. Paphiopedilums are notoriously difficult to reproduce by tissue culture.

To the amateur orchid grower, meristemming means that the finest orchids in the world, which a few years ago would have been sold for very high prices, are now available at a price well within reach.

Good health is achieved by providing the right environment for your orchids. Whether you grow your plants in a greenhouse, sun room or indoors, the aim is to recreate as nearly as possible the conditions under which the plant grows naturally. Although this may sound difficult to achieve, bearing in mind that orchids grow in many different environments throughout the world, in practice it is much easier than may at first appear. Although you would not expect your living room to resemble a tropical rainforest, the orchids which thrive in such conditions will be just as comfortable in a drier climate, provided that they get enough moisture at their roots to keep them plump and growing well; if so a satisfactory level of culture can be achieved. In a greenhouse, not as much emphasis is placed on watering as providing a moist atmosphere around the orchids. They will absorb as much moisture through their leaves and aerial roots from the atmosphere as a house-grown orchid will absorb from the damp compost in the pot. Watering should take priority over feeding, as it is of greater importance. Feeding can achieve results, but is not required in any great quantity.

Once you have created the right conditions in your greenhouse, you are more than halfway to growing orchids successfully. By becoming familiar with your plants and studying the way they grow in the conditions you provide you will very quickly come to understand their needs.

Another important factor in keeping your orchids healthy is to ensure that they remain free from pests and diseases. Indoors there is very little to worry about, although some pests such as red spider mite, scale insects or the lowly greenfly, all of which are present during the summer in trees and shrubs outside, can gain entry into your home and will find the dry conditions and your orchids very much to their liking. Under these conditions, they will rapidly multiply unless noticed and eradicated. The greenhouse grower is likely to be confronted with the same, and additional, pests, some of which will live in the greenhouse or be attracted by the warmth from outside. Such pests will have no difficulty in gaining an entry.

Healthy, pest-free orchids will reward the grower with an annual display of flowers, the climax to the season's loving care. The flower spikes and buds will need some care and attention if they are to be shown off at their best and enjoyed to the full. When all this has been achieved, it is a proud orchid grower who can show off his or her achievements. Many growers, having reached this stage, gain much satisfaction from exhibiting their orchids in flower. Starting with the local flower shows, where, if there are no classes specifically for orchids, they can be entered with ornamental greenhouse plants, and orchid society table shows, you will soon find your flowers are in demand by your local orchid society for collective exhibits at the larger horticultural exhibitions. Every year, one of the largest

PART IV
THE ART OF
ORCHID GROWING

exhibits of orchids at the world famous Chelsea Flower Show is staged by the Orchid Society of Great Britain. This collective display, expertly arranged and with magnificent specimens of many different orchids, is entirely made up of orchids grown by amateur growers with small, private collections. This magnificent achievement is matched by no other orchid society in the country, although nearly all hold their own annual exhibitions and cater for the beginner with monthly meetings at which both professional and amateur growers give lectures. In addition to the individual orchid society shows, which are usually advertised in the local press, there are nearly always some orchid exhibits by professional orchid nurserymen at the regular Royal Horticultural Society Shows in London. These shows offer an excellent opportunity to meet the experts and discuss any problems, as well as other enthusiasts who share your hobby. Joining your local orchid society is an excellent way of achieving greater enjoyment from your hobby, as well as increasing your knowledge. Comparing your own plants with those of other growers can tell you much about the condition of your plants. It can be difficult for a grower new to orchids to recognise signs of ill health before they have fully grasped the essential features of good health. This is something to be learnt as quickly as possible and is made all the easier by comparing orchids in other collections and commercial establishments.

The subsequent flowering of an orchid does not necessarily indicate that this is the result of good culture. Happily, this usually is the case, but it is also true that a sick plant, weakened beyond recovery by neglect, will, as its last act before dying, and in a last effort to perpetuate itself, use its remaining strength to produce flowers.

Therefore do not conclude that all must be well with a plant because it is flowering, and always remove flower spikes from either sick plants or very young seedlings. The latter will occasionally attempt to bloom before they are sufficiently mature, and this can weaken a small plant to the extent of delaying another flowering for two or three years while the plant slowly recovers from the strain. If you cannot bring yourself to remove the flower spike from a young plant when it first appears, nip out all but one bud and leave this to develop, cutting it immediately the flower is open. This will at least enable you to see the flower, and it will last a little time in water, while taking the strain from the plant.

Finally, it is not easy to kill orchid plants; they have great reserves and can be brought back from the brink of death by careful and expert care. Nevertheless, this is a long slow process, usually beyond the beginner, who would be advised to discard a sick plant, or find a more experienced grower to look after it, and replace with a healthy plant to try again.

WATERING

Spraying orchids is not the same as watering orchids which are growing in pots. These are two separate, and equally important, routine functions. Spraying is a beneficial operation carried out in the greenhouse which helps to keep foliage clean and free of dirt and dust, as well as helping to control certain pests such as red spider mite. It cools and freshens the leaves and aids moisture retention in the heat of the summer. It is natural for leaves to be regularly wetted; in their natural environment many orchids are subjected to a daily deluge during the rainy season. Cool winds quickly follow to dry excess moisture, and warm sunshine turns moisture into steam.

In the greenhouse, conditions are different. While we strive to copy nature's examples, moderation is the order of the day. Spraying is therefore carried out during the summer months only, when foliage will dry in the comparatively short time of ten minutes or half an hour, it should be done in the mornings, preferably sunny mornings when the temperature is rising and ventilators are open. By midday another spray can be given, and once again during the afternoon during periods of hot summer weather. On dull, rainy mornings it is better not to spray.

Spraying can be harmful if done at other times of the year. During the autumn and winter the water will be much colder and will lie on the leaf surface for twenty-four hours or more before drying up, as the humidity within the greenhouse on a cold, clammy winter's day will be naturally higher than in summer. During the spring, many orchids have young growths, partially developed, which will hold water in their furl of leaves. If left full of water overnight the result will be a rotting new growth. Also, the occasional bursts of bright

spring sunshine can easily burn tender young foliage; this danger is greatly increased if the foliage is wet. Spraying is therefore best commenced after the summer shading is in place, and only dappled sunlight is reaching the plants.

Even in summer not all orchids should be sprayed. Those which will definitely benefit are cymbidiums, odontoglossums, and other hard-leaved cool-growing genera such as coelogynes, encyclias and dendrobiums – basically, any orchid which retains its leaves over a number of years. The exception is the paphiopedilums. Their growths will quickly fill up with too much water, and again cause rot. This also applies to the warmer-growing phalaenopsis. All soft-leaved orchids and those which lose their leaves after one season, for example lycastes, pleiones, thunias, should not be overhead sprayed. Their soft foliage will quickly become spotted and spoiled. Spraying can also be useful in aiding the recovery of sick plants which have lost their roots, or newly repotted plants. Almost continuous spraying of the leaves will prevent moisture loss and slow dehydration until new roots have appeared.

Spraying over and above the plants on a hot summer's day will cause an immediate drop in temperature, cooling the leaves at the same time.

Cymbidiums will benefit from quite heavy spraying, using a fine mist nozzle the water can be sprayed over and through the plants until saturated. Water running down the leaves onto the pseudo-bulbs will do no harm during normal summer temperatures, when all surplus water will dry up within half an hour or so.

Damping-down is an important routine job which greatly benefits greenhouse-grown orchids. It is done to create that high humidity which is so important to the health of orchids. However, this humidity should be in balance with the temperature, and damping-down is done when the temperature is rising. During the winter months damping may be carried out once a week or so, and during the summer this might increase to once, twice, or even three times, daily. The floors, ground under the staging and staging areas should be sufficiently soaked so as to remain damp for several hours.

Where plants are growing mounted on bark or rafts on the side of the greenhouse wall, it could cause harm to remove each one for individual watering. Orchids growing in this way can more easily be damaged as they are more exposed. Many plants can be grouped together for convenience and to save space. The epiphytic varieties which grow best in this way usually require the same amount of watering, and as they are more well-drained than plants in pots it is virtually impossible to overwater them. It is, however, only too easy to *underwater* them! Therefore, regular spraying is essential to encourage the aerial roots, which are the whole aim of growing on bark, by which means the plant will take up its moisture. Spraying can be with plants on a vertical plane with just sufficient water remaining to moisten the base on which the plant is growing. While the plants are growing this spraying can be done once daily, and this should be enough to keep the plants evenly moist. Only if any plants accidentally get dried out need they be removed for a thorough dipping. The modest amount of liquid feed required by these plants may also be applied in the same way. The daily summer spray will probably be reduced to perhaps once or twice a week in winter for the orchids still growing. Those which enter a resting period should be left dry, and only sprayed if the pseudobulbs show signs of shrivelling.

The watering of orchids by can is ideal where just a few plants are kept. The water should be applied to the rim of the pot, using a long spouted can. Sufficient water should be given at one time to flood the whole surface twice. This will ensure that sufficient water has penetrated and been retained by the compost. Water should not be poured directly over the plant if there are young growths, where water may lodge, or if the plant is a *Paphiopedilum* or *Phalaenopsis* where water must be kept out of the centre of the plant. Any water which is accidentally spilt onto these plants should be emptied out. This problem of water laying in growths becomes more acute the smaller the greenhouse, particularly if there is no air movement. Large greenhouses create their own air movement when ventilators are open, or fans may be installed to increase this movement of air, which then ensures the drying up of surplus water before any harm can be done. Smaller greenhouses, without too much air movement where surface water may remain overnight will encourage rots. Liquid fertilisers or insecticides to be watered directly into the compost can also be given in this way.

Orchids growing indoors are usually watered by can, when the same remarks apply. Remember when you water to do it thoroughly, and give no more until the bark begins to dry out. The aim with all growing orchids is to keep the compost evenly moist to ensure a good steady growth.

Where many plants are to be watered the most sensible appliance is a long spouted lance fitted with a trigger and attached to a length of hosepipe. This may be fitted directly to the mains water supply or to an indoor water tank with a small pump. The trigger allows the exact amount of water onto each plant, and it is also possible to reach distant plants. Artificial liquid feed can also be supplied in the same way, and none need be wasted. This method of watering is very easy and allows you to water each plant individually and pass over those which do not require it.

A further method of watering orchids is to dip the pot in a bucket of water. This method ensures no wastage of water, and is therefore useful if water is in short supply, or if an insecticide or liquid fertiliser is being used. However, it is only practicable where a few plants are involved. Some orchids become far too large for constant lifting in and out of buckets. This application is most useful where a plant has suffered from underwatering and is shrivelling. Such a plant may be left with its pot submerged to just below the rim for up to half an hour, to ensure saturation of the compost. Small pots will float rather than remain submerged and sometimes the plant and compost will come loose from the pot and float free. It may therefore be necessary to place a small heavy object on the surface of the compost to hold it down. One advantage of watering this way is that the weight of the plant can be judged before and after watering, and this can be a useful guide. Newly repotted plants should not be dipped; they will require light watering with a can until new roots are established, and freshly potted compost will become loose and float free from the pot.

FEEDING

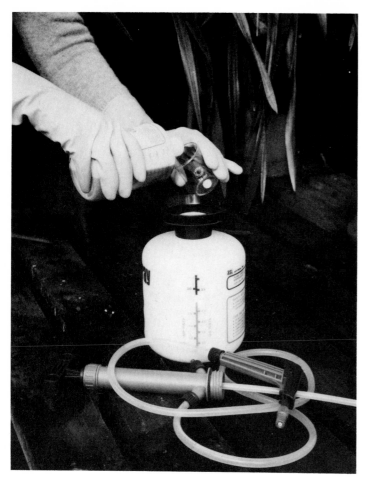

The feeding of orchids is less important than is usually supposed. That is not to say that artificial feeding is not beneficial, but it should be remembered that most of the orchids in our care are epiphytic plants and as such receive very little extra nutrients in their natural positions. Feeding should therefore be in moderation only, and should be given in accordance with the growth cycle of the plant, bearing in mind that orchids are for the most part slow-growing, long-lived plants.

Feeding can commence as spring arrives. As the extension of daylight hours and the higher temperature cause the plants to become active after their winter's rest, feeding is given on a fortnightly basis to start with, using a weak solution carefully measured according to manufacturer's instructions. As spring develops into summer and the plants enter their maximum growing period, the frequency of each feed may be increased to once a week or even ten days, depending upon how often the plant is watered. As summer ends, feeding is reduced to be discontinued for the winter. Feeding directly to the pot is good, provided that two waterings without feed are given in between. This is to prevent a build-up of salts in the compost, and to ensure that excess chemicals are washed from the pot.

Feeding directly to the pot is the easiest way if you are growing in the home. Under greenhouse culture foliar feeding is perhaps easier, and less wasteful of feed where many plants are concerned.

Experienced growers can easily work out a feeding programme based on their own knowledge. Beginners would be advised to use a phosphate or nitrogen-based feed, very diluted as described above.

The feeding of orchids growing in a uniform batch is best accomplished by spraying over the foliage using a fine nozzle which can be turned on or off at will. The result of foliar feeding in this way will be to keep the foliage a good healthy green and can permit extra light to be given as a result. Growth will speed up, and this will be particularly noticeable on young plants. Foliar feeding should be done in the early part of the day, as with all spraying, to allow time for the foliage to dry off before nightfall. If the plants are regularly overhead sprayed, leave dry for a day after foliar feeding. This will give the plants time to absorb the feed before any surplus is washed from the leaves at subsequent sprayings with water.

It is possible to overfeed orchids, and this will normally show up as burn marks in the form of black streaking or mottling over the leaf surface. Care should also be taken not to feed on very bright mornings, when again burning could be caused by the sun on wet leaves.

Young plants, in particular, must be encouraged to grow at a steady rate, and this can be encouraged by steady feeding. This is different to the feed given to, say, a tomato crop, where a short, fast burst of growth and energy is desired. Newly repotted orchids must be fed very lightly indeed until a new root system has formed.

Not all orchids are suited to liquid foliar feeding. Those with soft, annual foliage will quickly spoil if they are sprayed at all. Lycastes, pleiones, phaius and thunias are a few examples of orchids which should not be sprayed. They can be fed directly through the roots. This food can be the same liquid food as already mentioned, or, if you prefer the old-fashioned method of using an organic substance, pieces of old dried cow manure are as good today as they were a hundred years ago. In those early days of orchid culture growers would water the whole ground surface of the greenhouse with liquid cow manure to increase the CO_2 in the atmosphere.

Small pieces of dried cow manure can be placed on the surface of the compost, and the goodness will be gradually washed down to the roots during waterings. Only orchids with a sound root system should be fed in this way. With newly repotted plants, wait until the new growth is developing well until the feed is applied, as can be seen here. Cow manure will attract moss flies and other small pests which lay their eggs in the pieces. The grubs which hatch can be troublesome, as they break down the manure faster than is required. A watering with an insecticide should control these pests. Other manures such as horse or chicken are too strong and should not be used.

Less odorous forms of slow-release feeding are available and suitable for orchids. These usually come in granule form, and again they should not be overdone, but applied during the late spring when plants are growing strongly with developing growth and root systems. Usually one teaspoon of granules is quite sufficient for an 8- or 10-in (20- or 25-cm) pot. Once sprinkled over the surface they will last the whole season, and no other form of feeding will be necessary. This is a clean and easy way to feed, and is particularly useful with indoor plants. The advantage of this method of feeding is that the fertiliser is released slowly, over a period of time, and works its way down to the roots, with little danger of overfeed or burning being caused to the root system. For this reason the slow-release fertiliser should not be included at the base of the plant when repotting, or mixed in with the compost, where you cannot be certain how much food each individual plant has received.

Whatever form of feeding is preferable, it is important to feed only healthy plants, which are growing strongly and have a good root system. Do not feed sick plants which have lost their roots, and do not feed resting plants. Feed during the spring and into late summer months, and discontinue throughout the winter when the daylight hours are short and there is insufficient light to warrant feeding. Finally, with slow-release feeding, it is always a good practice to keep a record on the plant's label of the date the fertiliser was applied.

Mice are not generally thought of as a serious pest to orchids, yet, surprisingly, a survey has shown that mice and rats can cause a considerable amount of damage to both plants and flowers. Seldom seen during the day, the grower is usually unaware of their presence until the damage is discovered, by which time a family of field or house mice may have taken up residence in the greenhouse. They are attracted by the warmth and promise of food at the onset of winter. If not actually nesting in the greenhouse they will travel to and fro each night, therefore you may not necessarily find a nest. The usual means of entry are under ill-fitting doors or ventilators, or other small holes in the lower framework. Rats, which must also be considered and which can create even more havoc, will burrow underneath the foundations to gain entry.

Mice seem to be attracted to pollen, which they find highly nutritious. They will ascend the tallest of flower spikes, even detecting pollen in tightly-closed buds, where they will nibble their way through the side of the bud, to remove the pollen for their feast. Open flowers are more vulnerable, and the mice will even tear off the pouches of paphiopedilums in their eagerness. The thick fleshy aerial roots of phalaenopsis are another example of their preferences, as also are the pseudobulbs on very young and tender plants.

If you suspect that mice have been at work, one of the first noticeable signs will be the reddening of the lip on *Cymbidium* flowers.

Close examination will reveal small teeth marks on the column and unopened buds. A further look will confirm that the pollen is missing.

In a small greenhouse a quick check should soon tell you whether the mice have nested; the nest should not be too difficult to find and eliminate. They will nest in warm, dry corners, particularly if any rubbish is allowed to accumulate under the benches. All holes should immediately be blocked to prevent further intrusion. In a larger greenhouse, with inaccessible corners, poison may be the surest way, but this can result in a lingering odour after the mice have been killed. Humane traps are an alternative and successful method of control.

Rats, being larger, can do even more harm and be more destructive. They have similar tastes to mice, and will munch their way through whole pseudobulbs, which can be an invaluable source of food to them during the lean winter months.

Putting right the damage can take time. Where flowers have been ruined, the grower can only wait for the next season. Chewed roots will invariably grow again, branching a little way behind the damaged end which will quickly heal by itself. Keep an eye on damaged pseudobulbs which have been gnawed, and provided that the wound is dry healing will take place naturally, leaving only a scar. It is important to prevent water getting into the wound, and an application of sulphur will ensure that it is kept dry.

The pests which attack orchid plants can be roughly divided into those naturally indigenous to our gardens and those tropical pests which have been introduced with importations of plants over many years. Although this latter group could not survive cold winters out of doors, in the warmth of our greenhouses they thrive.

Scale insects belong to this second group, as also do mealy bugs, which at first glance bear a close resemblance to woolly scale and are often confused with it. Closer examination reveals that the two are quite different. Under its woolly covering the mealy bug is a pinkish mite, very soft and easily removed. Woolly scale is a small white insect under its protective coat. Other scale insects are quite different. Most are round, or mussle-shaped, and all are covered by a shell-like membrane, which may be soft or surprisingly hard. Their colour can vary from white to dark brown.

There are as many species of scale insects as there are parts of the plant they will attack and attach themselves to. Mostly, scale will be found around the base of a plant, even below the compost level. On cattleyas they inhabit the rhizome and pseudobulbs, entirely unseen under the bracts and sheathing. If unchecked they creep up from the base onto the undersides of the leaves. Less often, a few scattered scale adhere to the topside of the leaf.

Woolly scale thrives in hot, dry conditions and will attack all types of orchids. It is one of the most familiar scale and also one of the most persistent. Usually attacking the base of the plant, it can build up into large colonies where it destroys dormant 'eyes', the future growths, causes leaves to turn prematurely yellow, and eventually kills a plant. The first sign is often the yellowing foliage. Cymbidiums are particularly vulnerable to woolly scale as illustrated. Here a bad infestation has carpeted the leafless pseudobulbs as well as the new growth on the right. Higher up on the leaves can be seen the start of a new occupation with a few scattered insects visible on the leaves. On the central new growth both male and the larger female insects can be seen.

A plant which has become as badly infected as this is probably best thrown away. It will take a long time to completely eradicate the scale, and the plant has already been greatly weakened, and has lost many leaves prematurely.

There are various fairly safe insecticides available. Among the best and easiest to use are systemics which can be sprayed or applied while watering. This insecticide is retained in the sap stream of the plant and renders it poisonous to most insects and mites. For scale insects systemic can be most effective, but it is still necessary to clean off the scale first.

A quick and easy method of controlling scale insects is brushing with a toothbrush or paintbrush dipped in methylated spirits. This will loosen even the hardest scale. All bracts should be peeled back and will reveal more scale. Because of its penetrating nature the spirit will affect those parts of the plant out of reach. Some virulent forms of scale can be resistant to methylated spirits and it may be necessary to repeat the cleaning several times before the pest is successfully eradicated. As with all insecticides there is the danger of burning young growth – soft-leaved orchids are particularly vulnerable – and immediately after using methylated spirits it should be rinsed thoroughly with clean water.

Alternatively, use nothing stronger than luke-warm water to which has been added a little washing-up liquid for dislodging the scale. Affected plants should be separated from all others and inspected frequently over several months. Usually a plant that has been cleaned of scale and appears free from it may become re-infested up to several years later. Such is the resilient nature of this unwelcome pest.

Greenfly are common in gardens throughout most of the year and will find their way onto the buds or flowers of orchids, where they suck the sap causing deformities and bud drop. They will also appear on new growths, and are difficult to control with insecticides which can cause more harm by burning these soft parts. The easiest method is to remove them by washing off with slightly soapy water on a soft artist's brush. When young flower spikes and buds are growing, check daily for greenfly and prevent a build-up which will need a systemic insecticide.

Large colonies of greenfly on open flowers are hard to control by washing off. If left for any length of time they secrete a sugary substance which shows up as sticky patches. On leaves which are not being regularly overhead sprayed, these quickly develop a black sooty mould. By this time the flowers may have been removed from the plant, making it difficult to define the cause of the problem. Wherever this black mould, or a clear sticky area, is seen, greenfly should be looked for. The substance is easily washed off with water and a sponge.

Vine weevil is a common indigenous pest which easily finds its way into a greenhouse. Dormant by day, it will emerge at night actively to attack flower petals. The larvae exist in the compost where they can cause damage to the root system. Both larva and adult are long-lived and difficult to kill, being resistant to most insecticides. Beetles can be tracked down individually and destroyed. During the day it may be found under the compost. Modern bark composts unfortunately seem to provide an ideal daytime home for this pest.

Of all the seemingly inoffensive insects which come into the greenhouse, it is the large bumble bees which are most harmful to orchid flowers. During warm spells in the early spring, the queen bumble bees emerge from their hibernation at a time when the only flowers available are vulnerable *Cymbidium* blooms. The bright sunshine makes it necessary to open ventilators and thus allow the bees in, attracted by the powerful scent. The bumble bee performs pollination causing the premature death of the flower: do not be tempted to sow seed from such a haphazard pollination. To avoid trouble ventilators should be covered with a fine gauze.

Caterpillars are seldom associated with orchids, but when they do attack the amount of damage carried out in one night can be tremendous. Hiding by day down among the leaves, or in the surface compost where they cannot be seen, they climb up to the buds at night to feed with a voracious appetite on the delicate tissue of the potential blooms. The best method of control is to make nightly patrols with a torch to pick off the caterpillars. The damage they cause is similar to that of slugs, the difference being that there are no tell-tale silver trails.

The common woodlouse, so plentiful in the garden, will also be found in dirty greenhouses. Woodlice thrive on decomposing material. Once established, they will gain access to plants by entering through the drainage hole and residing in the compost, where they will hasten the decomposition of the bark compost. In some cases they can also attack young roots. They are not easy to eradicate but can be controlled with a powder which should be dusted around the floor and places of entry. A high standard of cleanliness achieved by the use of Jeyes Fluid in the greenhouse will keep them at bay.

Of all pests which attack orchids, the common slug is undoubtedly the most persistent. Unfortunately good orchid conditions actively encourage this pest, which will attack any part of any plant providing it is sufficiently tender. Slugs are particularly keen on developing flower spikes and buds. As with most other pests slugs will enter a greenhouse through any small holes and cracks in the glass or by hitching a lift on shoes during a wet evening visit!

This is a nocturnal pest, only occasionally seen during the day. Often the offending mollusc can be found lurking just beneath the surface of the compost, otherwise a torchlight search after dark is almost certain to reveal the culprit.

On *Cymbidium* spikes the slug will spend the day hidden within the sheathing which covers the lower part of the spike. Shining a torch through the sheaths at night will often reveal this hiding place. Slugs will climb any length of spike to find the buds; length of stem is no protection!

For all-round effective control, prevention is better than cure. Slug pellets can be regularly sprinkled around outside and inside the greenhouse, covering the floor, under staging, surface of staging and pots. Any pellets placed in the pots near to a growth should be

cleaned up within a few days before moulds have a chance to grow and cause further trouble. Pellets are far preferable to powdered bait which will leave permanent marks on the foliage if contact is made. Liquid poison can be used if preferred and should be sprayed over the plants, giving a blanket cover but avoiding the buds. Liquid poison is a contact killer and can therefore be more effective. Ideally it should be used regularly, alternating with applications of pellets.

One of the oldest and most successful methods of protecting flower spikes (right) is to wrap a small wad of cotton wool around the spike and supporting cane, well above the compost. Provided that this is kept dry no slug will be able to cross it. The early orchid growers learnt this by observing that plants with furry stems were not attacked. Another method of those times, which still works today, is the famous 'slug pub', which is a saucer of beer, which slugs cannot resist. They will be found drowned the following day. Another means of protecting your special prize plant is to place its pot on an upturned pot standing in a tray of water. Provided that you can be certain you have not marooned the offending slug on your island, the plant should be quite safe.

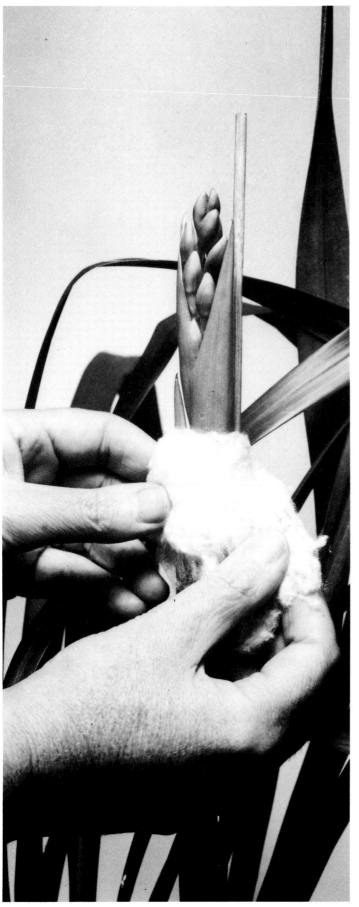

The common garden snail will cause as much damage as the slugs, and can be controlled by the same methods. The very large snails because of their size are often unable to find a large enough entry hole. There is another snail, much smaller, more persistent and which is of more concern to orchid growers. This is a small, flat, dark brown species, commonly known as the 'bush' or 'garlic' snail; the latter name arises because of the pungent odour of garlic which it emits when disturbed or squashed. For most of the time these minute snails remain out of sight beneath the compost, where they feed mostly on algae and mosses. They also appear to be attracted to new *Cattleya* growths where they are seen to be feeding on the nectar created by it. The only damage they are likely to do to orchids is restricted to very young seedlings whose roots they will destroy.

Control by poison is not easy; they are not attracted to slug bait and the liquid killer does not seem to affect them. Again we have to turn to an old-fashioned remedy, the snails will congregate beneath slices of apple on the compost where they can be dealt with the following day. This method can be repeated as often as necessary, but the apple should be replaced fresh each day.

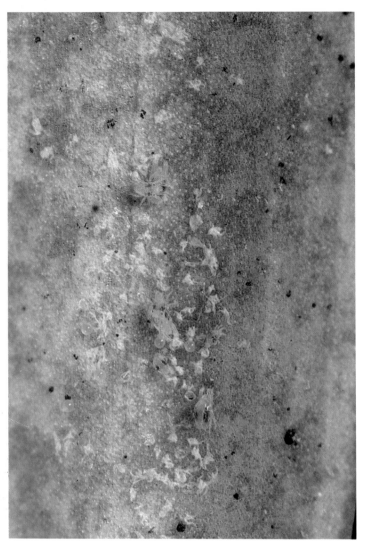

No pest is more devastating and yet can remain unnoticed for greater lengths of time than red spider mite. These minute creatures are neither spiders nor are they red. They belong to a large family of mites, many of which are so small that they can hardly be seen with the naked eye. The ones which attack orchids are usually yellowish or whitish and can be seen on the underside of the leaves with a magnifying glass. At first the damage is more obvious than the pest itself. A white silvery sheen on the underside of leaves is an indication of the damage done. It is the result of the leaf cells being sucked dry and dying. As the pest spreads the damage is enormous. The above illustration has been enlarged many times to show the red spider colony. The adult mite is largest and as it grows it sheds its skin. The juveniles' white husks can also be seen. They do not have a larval stage as other insects, but lay eggs which hatch rapidly. A common pest in our gardens, mostly during the summer months, they breed in hot dry weather. They are controlled by the natural elements of wind, rain and cold winters. Once established in the totally artificial environment of the greenhouse where no such natural control exists they will breed unchecked. For their small size they are extremely active and spread easily from plant to plant. Once a colony is well established the mites will spin a fine web over the leaves and flower buds. This webbing helps to protect them from water and insecticide.

Hard-leaved orchids such as the cattleyas are seldom worried by red spider mite. It is the softer-leaved orchids such as odontoglossums and miltonias which may be attacked from time to time, but it is the cymbidiums which are most at risk. On these plants the pest can build up quickly amongst the dense foliage. By comparing two cymbidium leaves (above right), it is easy to see the damage done. The left-hand leaf is clean and free from the pest. The underside of the leaf is a good dark green. The leaf on the right shows the devastation caused. Soft-leaved dendrobiums can be badly affected to the extent that all the leaves die. They will turn a silvery white before becoming yellow and dropping off. This devastation, even on a deciduous orchid, can result in the death of the plant. There is also a smaller form of this mite called pacific mite or false red spider mite. This is not often seen in Britain or Europe but it will attack phalaenopsis causing deep pitting and scarring of the foliage. The control of mites may be carried out in various ways. Over the years a number of insecticides or microcides have been developed. Some of these have been withdrawn from the market as being too dangerous to be used. In recent years there has been much experimentation with a predatory mite. This is another form of mite which feeds on the red spider mite; this is termed biological control. These predatory mites are commercially produced in large quantities, and sold by mail order. Released onto your own plants the predators will quickly

devour and bring under control the red spider. As they will soon eat themselves out of food, it is necessary to re-introduce the predator on a proper programmed basis. Unfortunately, this form of control is more effective on certain plants than others and it has not been very successful on orchids for reasons not fully understood. The best method of control for the amateur grower is to spray with one of the systemic microcides available today and to sponge the foliage regularly to keep the pest to a minimum. A good humid atmosphere and regular spraying of the foliage particularly in summer months will be more effective than anything else. However, during the winter when days are short and there are many plants in flower, the grower naturally keeps the atmosphere slightly drier and does not spray cymbidiums as much as in the summer, so it is at this time of the year that the pest is likely to gain a foothold.

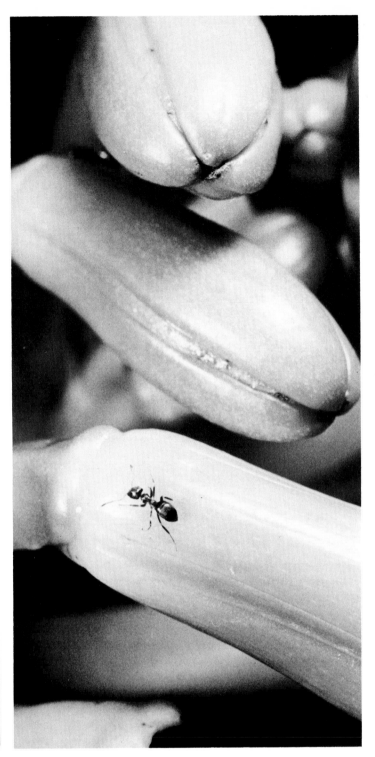

Cockroaches are an old-fashioned pest. In a modern, clean greenhouse you are unlikely to come across them. Nevertheless, they can cause damage to every soft part of a plant, including roots, growths and flowers. Detection is not easy, as they are nocturnal and can run very fast. Eradication by the method of soaking the areas they are known to inhabit with Jeyes Fluid is often best; otherwise put down poison out of doors in cool temperate climates.

Ants have always been connected with orchids, and in the wild are found in large nests living in the clumps of some orchids. On cultivated orchids they are attracted by the nectar that exudes from the base of the buds before the flowers are open. Our illustration shows *Vanilla* buds secreting nectar from the back of the flower buds. By cleaning up the sugary secretion, the ants prevent moulds from growing, and therefore are not to be discouraged. If, however, they nest or encourage aphids, scale and mealy bug by their strange process of milking them, they can be discouraged by using ant powder.

Moss flies are small insects whose whitish larvae cause more concern than the adult flies. These larvae are seldom seen as they are extremely small and live entirely beneath the compost. They are a common fly in the garden but generally go unnoticed due to their size. In the greenhouse often when you are watering the adults are disturbed and are seen flitting about the surface of the compost between the plants. They have a fast breeding rate, the eggs turning into small white maggots. These live on decomposing plant material, bark, peat, moss and other vegetative compost. They are also attracted to the roots of young plants. In large quantities they can break the compost down at an alarming rate, causing it to become muddy. The adults, which are poor fliers, seldom leave the immediate area where they have been breeding, which makes it easy to detect where the larvae are to be found. The flies can be killed with an ordinary greenhouse aerosol but the larvae are much harder to destroy. Watering the plant with a weak solution of insecticide will usually flush them out. Due to the fast breeding cycle there are always eggs or pupae which have not been killed. It is important, particularly in hot weather when breeding is even faster, to repeat the control at regular intervals. By killing the adult fly, you will have broken the cycle and the infestation will be reduced to an acceptable level. Orchid growers have always been aware of this pest, as well as other small insects such as springtails, which can be particularly troublesome in the seedling house.

Springtails are mostly to be found underneath the pots. They are small, whitish, extremely agile insects which can jump considerably high for their size, a feat which gives them their common name. They live in the base of pots and in large numbers cause the same problems as moss flies. Their control is similar to that used for moss flies. An early method of control of moss flies still used today is to place a plant of *Pinguicula cordata* (above) in the vicinity. This is an insectivorous plant, with large fleshy leaves covered with minute hairs. Each hair forms a carpet of sticky substance on which the flies soon become stuck. They are broken down and dissolve into the tissue of the leaf. These plants also make an attractive addition to the greenhouse as they have pretty, long-lasting, pink blooms. However, insectivorous plants are very susceptible to any form of fertiliser or insecticide, and should you grow them amongst your seedlings you will need to remove the *Pinguicula* before spraying with aerosols.

DISEASES AND DISORDERS

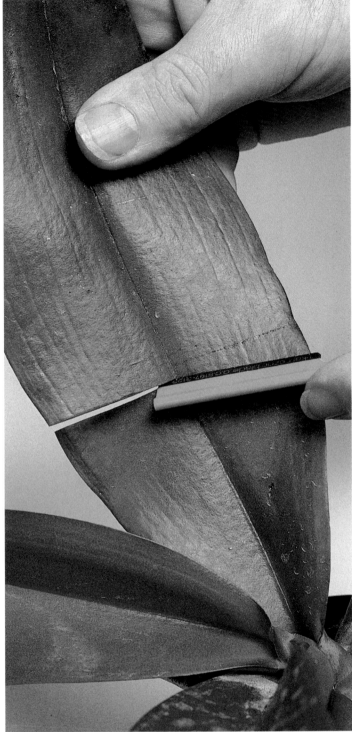

Diseases of the foliage can attack many of the soft-leaved orchids particularly in winter when there is always a danger of the temperature dropping below the minimum required. Bacteria and fungi can attack suddenly. The warm-loving phalaenopsis which require a minimum winter night temperature of at least 65° F (18° C) easily fall prey. *Pseudomonas cattleyae* disease can break out rapidly on the top or underside of the leaf where large brown watery patches appear and spread with alarming ferocity until the whole plant is enveloped within a few days. Where the infection is bad all infected plants should be destroyed.

When brown wet spot (*Pseudomonas cattleyae*) is caught early, the leaf can be cut through with a sharp sterile instrument well below the affected area. In our illustration the disease has struck mostly on the underside of the leaf but within a few days would have quickly spread. This plant can still be saved, providing that treatment is carried out at once. Needless to say, all dead material removed from the plant should be taken out of the greenhouse and disposed of properly to prevent further spread of the disease.

After the diseased part of the leaf has been cut away make sure there is no spread of the infection onto the clean part of the leaf remaining. The thick *Phalaenopsis* leaves contain moisture and care should be taken to prevent any infection of the wound. A paintbrush can be used to dust the severed edge with Flowers of Sulphur as an antiseptic and to help to dry the wound. The life of the plant may well have been saved and if the new centre leaf has not been damaged by the disease, the plant stands a good chance of being grown out of this disfigurement.

A *Phalaenopsis* which has been treated for brown wet spot can be placed in front of a small electric fan for half an hour to dry up the cut rapidly. This equipment is now commonplace in an orchid house. This treatment is only a form of first aid. The best method is prevention of the disease occurring in the first place; and where a hygienic greenhouse is maintained, and the proper temperatures adhered to, these diseases will not occur. They appear mostly where low temperatures and high humidity are combined during cold months.

Cattleya Wilt or Fusarium Wilt (*Fusarium oxysporum*) is a condition which causes the leaves to hang limply in a severely shrivelled state (left). It is not a disease or the result of an insect infestation, as is often thought, but a condition triggered by a number of cultural faults. The effect can be the same with several different causes. This particular plant is suffering from severe drought over a very long period. When resting, cattleyas can remain dry for several weeks at a time without harm. If, however, the same plant is kept too dry during its growing season, it is forced to draw on its own reserves with drastic results. Overwatering could have a similar effect, creating the same symptoms as underwatering. A plant that has been severely overwatered will have lost its root system and the foliage will droop and become dehydrated. The best solution for such plants is to repot immediately and keep in a humid atmosphere. Light regular spraying will prevent further moisture loss from the leaves. After a new season's growth has been started and a new root system established it is possible to bring some life back to the old shrivelled pseudobulbs. Recovery will be slow, and the grower must consider whether the time spent is worthwhile. It will certainly be several seasons before a plant in this condition will regain full health and flowering ability.

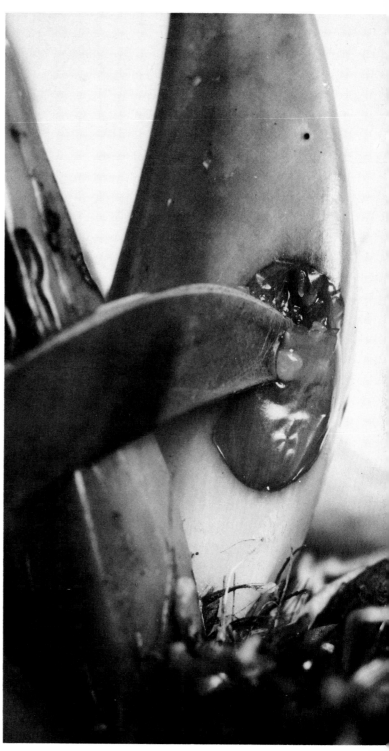

Orchids with soft pseudobulbs can suffer a wet bacterial infection similar to that experienced on *Phalaenopsis* leaves. These infections occur mostly on the recently completed pseudobulbs and are more often isolated to one, but will emerge anew each year on the season's pseudobulb. Alternatively, they may spread through the plant, killing it completely. Our illustration (opposite right) shows a badly-infected pseudobulb which is one season old. The condition can be treated by cutting out the rot. A sharp penknife should be sterilised by passing it through the flame of a lighter (above).

Lance the wound on the new *Oncidium* pseudobulb with a sterilised knife, and having cut through the skin scrape away all brown or black infected material until the green soft tissue can be seen. The blade should be constantly wiped clean and reflamed to prevent infecting the clean fleshy part of the pseudobulb. Sometimes the watery area will be found to have penetrated quite deeply into the pseudobulb, and when all is cleaned out the size of the hole is surprising.

When the wound has been prepared and all the rotten portion removed, it should be patted dry with a paper tissue and swabbed with methylated spirits. This will quickly evaporate without burning the plant. Once the wound is completely dry it may be stood in front of an electric fan to ensure complete dryness. This will help to prevent a secondary infection of the exposed tissue. Orchids which can become infected in this way are many of the bulbous varieties. The one illustrated is *Oncidium leucochilum*, which seems more prone to the disease, as also are hybrids from it. Sometimes *Pseudomonas cattleyae* will stop entirely by itself to remain as a dried-up black scab on the side of the pseudobulb. The cause is usually a culture fault where low temperature and high humidity have occurred together, or where a resting plant has been overwatered. It follows that these problems usually occur in the winter months rather than in the summer when there is plenty of fresh air and strong light which are the best defences against these diseases. The infection can also be started by a slug eating a hole in the side of the pseudobulb, allowing the disease to enter the plant. The disease invariably comes suddenly, without warning, and starts as a mere spot the size of a pin head. Therefore, the earlier it is treated the smaller the hole.

Having thoroughly dried the wound and satisfied yourself that there is little likelihood of it spreading further, the plant should be laid on its side to have the wound completely packed with Flowers of Sulphur. This will act as an antiseptic and stop reinfection occurring. The sulphur itself will not harm the plant, though it does look somewhat unsightly. After a week or two, when healing has started, the surplus sulphur can be dusted off. Sufficient will remain attached to the area to prevent it getting wet when watering. However, during the first few weeks after the treatment has been carried out, the plant should be kept dry, and a 'hospital' shelf at the end of the greenhouse is always a good idea. After the plant has dried out and the pseudobulb allowed to shrivel slightly, you will find that the wound has completely healed. Although unsightly, and preventing the plant from winning prizes in a flower show, the orchid will have been saved to grow and flower again another day.

The packing of wounds with sulphur is the best remedy whatever the cause. Fresh slug holes in pseudobulbs, and damage which occurs when a plant is accidentally dropped onto the floor, can all be treated in the same way. However, if you discover an old, dried-up hole, which is obviously causing no threat to the plant, there is little point in plugging this with sulphur.

Orchids can sustain various marks or spots to their foliage, bearing in mind that some orchids, such as cymbidiums, retain their leaves for five or six years. It is quite possible that during this time they become marked or damaged. It takes a trained eye to decide whether these marks are a serious infection or something that is of no consequence, such as natural deterioration of old foliage. Sunburn, mainly in the spring, is one cause. After the long winter period of little sunshine the plant has become soft and unused to bright light.

It is not uncommon for the tips of some orchid leaves to die and turn black. If this die-back does not spread it is probably nothing more than old age. This happens more on cymbidiums and odontoglossums. If this occurs on the young growths or new leaves then the cause must be looked into. It could be the result of poor culture, or possibly a combination of cold, damp conditions. Otherwise, overwatering or exposure to bright sunlight are other possible causes. Often cutting off the dead tips will prevent the die-back from running further down the leaf.

Virus disease in orchids can occur in almost any genus, showing up as ugly black markings. Not all black marks on foliage, however, are due to virus. Often they are initially caused by poor cultural conditions, which can lead to a virus infection. Virus is usually distinguishable by its definite semi-circular or diamond pattern. There is no cure and the plant should be disposed of. Infection is spread by sap-sucking insects or pruning knives used for cutting dead leaves. For this reason all cutting instruments should be regularly sterilised.

Virus disease attacks and kills the leaf cells allowing a secondary infestation of bacteria to set in. It is this secondary infection which causes the black, darkened areas. The only way to make a positive identification of a virus-infected plant is to have it identified in a laboratory where particular tests can be carried out. Making sure that all plants introduced to your collection are initially clean and free from any form of pest or disease will help to prevent its introduction into your collection. Good husbandry is preferable to having to treat any form of disease.

Where seedlings are grown in trays or community pots it is important to inspect them daily for leaf loss. Even under the most hygienic conditions seedlings will damp off for no apparent reason and a certain loss is always expected amongst young plants. To prevent this spreading, and killing the whole contents of a tray, a daily inspection is necessary to remove any transparent or yellow leaves to prevent contact with the rest of the stock. Regular preventive treatment with fungicide is a good idea, but great care should be taken as some fungicides contain growth inhibitors.

Orchid blooms which have been open for several weeks will often show some natural age spotting. However, if spotting occurs within a short time of the flower opening, the cause is usually a combination of high humidity and low temperature. The spotting will quickly spread, prematurely ageing the flower. It is most frequently seen on softer flowers, cattleyas being an example. Any plants in flower should be kept in a slightly drier atmosphere and watering reduced slightly. Orchids in the home will often last longer than in a moist greenhouse. The same conditions will also cause the pollen masses to rot, the pollen cap to turn black and the flower to die.

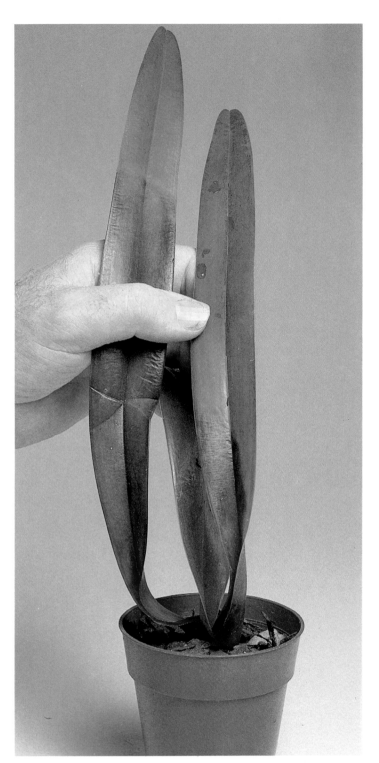

Basal rot (also known as Southern Blight) in young growths is caused by the disease *Sclerotium rolfsii* and can be directly related to water, either through overwatering or water remaining in the growth, or cold and damp conditions. Hence the rot starts at the base of the plant and runs up through the foliage. It is more likely to occur on a weakened plant. The rotting growth should be completely removed at its base, cutting away with a clean, sharp knife. The area should be dusted with sulphur and the plant kept on the dry side until a further new growth appears to replace the lost one.

Basal rot is where the plant turns brown at its base, and the rot progresses through the plant. It is caused by overwatering, particularly when combined with low temperatures. Paphiopedilums seem particularly susceptible, and although the outer leaves may appear healthy if the centre of the crown has rotted the plant is doomed. Water lying in the centre of the growth will easily cause rot. Once the infection has established itself it can quickly spread so an infected plant should be instantly removed.

CARE OF PLANTS

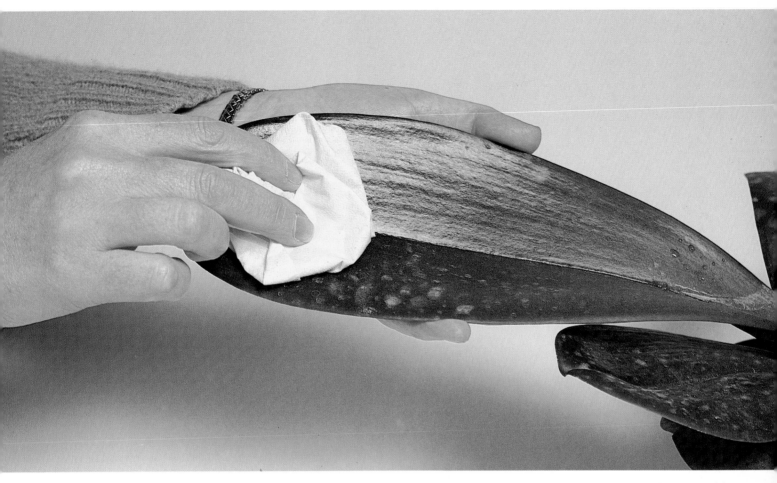

The care you take in keeping your orchids clean and tidy is just as important a factor in their culture as are temperature, watering and light requirements. When these factors have been satisfactorily dealt with and you are happy with the conditions you are providing, you can turn your attention to the plants themselves. Simply by handling your plants daily you will learn more about the way they grow and flower. A routine examination can start by gently tapping a plant out of its pot and observing the root system. If you keep a record, a glance at its label will tell you when it was last repotted. You then have some idea of how the root system has progressed in that time. In the summer you should see a mass of healthy white roots, each ending in a green growing tip. These same roots in the winter will appear to have no growing tips as they have ceased to grow for a period. The compost between the roots, where it can be seen, should be neither dust-dry nor soaking wet; just nice and moist with a pleasant 'woodland' aroma. If you are satisfied that all is well with the roots, you can be sure all is well with the plant, and the pot is carefully replaced with no disturbance at all to the plant. If this examination had revealed a mass of blackened, dead roots the plants would have been removed to the potting bench for immediate attention. Apart from an occasional examination, roots require no other attention than is given to them at repotting time. Aerial roots, of course, can be examined daily with a glance.

Having returned the plant to its pot, take a long look at the state of the leaves, which should be green and healthy. The shade of green varies according to the type, for example a light green on lycastes, a dark green on phalaenopsis. Both are healthy. A yellowish, sickly green could indicate over-exposure to light (in the summer) or lack of nourishment caused either by poor compost, which should have already been noticed, or by the need for some artificial feed. Alternatively, the yellowing of the foliage may be nothing more than the plant approaching its dormant period. This is determined by whether the plant is an evergreen or deciduous type. The occasional yellow leaf is to be expected from time to time. Phalaenopsis usually carry between three and five leaves, losing one leaf from the base of the plant every other year or so. The large flat leaves of phalaenopsis will gather dirt (in the form of a residue caused by heavily calcified or limy water from artesian wells, or a white crust remaining after liquid food or insecticide has been applied) and dust, where the plants are growing indoors. Regular sponging will ensure a cleaner, healthier leaf, and greatly improve the look of the plant by its shine. Dusty leaves can be cleaned with a dry paper tissue, laid flat on the leaf at the centre of the plant and drawn across its surface to the tip while supporting the leaf from underneath. Residue will be more persistent, and a damp sponge used in the same way will be more effective, drawing it across the leaf without 'scrubbing', which could crack a leaf. If you are fortunate to have a soft water supply you will find that your leaves keep much cleaner, and less cleaning will be necessary. However, orchids grown as house plants should be sponged at least once a week to remove the dust, and damp spongeing on a daily basis will take the place of spraying in a greenhouse.

The leafless pseudobulbs of cymbidiums are completely covered by the bracts which are all that remains of the base of the leaves which have been shed. They have a natural break-off point where the old yellow leaves separate and fall naturally from the plant. This point is clearly seen in the above picture. This leaves the pseudobulbs sheathed with the stumpy, unsightly bracts which are quite sharp and can easily scratch the unwary grower. The bracts are removed from time to time to improve the appearance of the plant and prevent it harbouring pests such as scale and mealy bug which can build up into large unseen colonies. Starting from the outside split the old bracts at their points and strip them down each side of the pseudobulb, being careful not to damage any small flower spikes or new growth at the base. They should peel off quite easily leaving a clean pseudobulb with the green base showing. Only dried bracts should be removed in this way. Do not attempt to remove the base of leaves which are still green as they appear on odontoglossums.

Cymbidium leaves are long and numerous and can be cleaned individually by supporting the base of each leaf with the finger and thumb and using a tissue or sponge to draw upwards removing all dirt, dust and any red spider mite in one movement (right). Regular treatment like this with either a wet or dry tissue will help to keep the leaves in a clean and healthy condition. The sponge can be seeped in a

solution of insecticide to kill any insect pests which may be active on the plant. This practice should be carried out several times a year and particularly before exhibiting the plant. This method of cleaning the leaves should not be tried on young or immature growths as the soft fleshy leaves at the centre are easily pulled out. After cleaning one leaf, search for red spider mite among the dirt and dust. These are more easily seen on a white paper tissue than on the leaves.

Growers with little experience are rightly concerned about water remaining on orchid foliage. Under good growing conditions this surplus water will soon evaporate and cause no harm. In their natural environment the growths of paphiopedilums are regularly filled with water after rain. However, in a small greenhouse or indoors where there is little air movement, you may be concerned and should remove this moisture or any dirt and dust particles that have collected in the centre growth with a small camel-hair brush (far right), which is ideal for paphiopedilums, phalaenopsis and other plants with centres. This surface water can cause harm when the temperature is low and may result in a chill to the plant, causing a rot. Water can also be harmful to flower buds growing from the centre and can be the cause of damping-off, possibly followed by a bacterial infection. No harm will come to the plants with water-filled centres unless the conditions are wrong.

Appearances matter, and if your cymbidiums suffer leaves broken or damaged at their base they will look unsightly. This damage can easily be repaired (left) and if it is treated immediately the repair will restore the leaves to their former positions without support. The alternative is to remove them by splitting them at their centre lengthways and pulling them downwards away from the pseudobulb. Make sure there are no flower spikes or young growths which could be damaged at the base. Only remove the leaves if on an older pseudobulb, and if the plant can spare them. Leaves on a leading pseudobulb should not be taken away.

The broken leaves on a *Cymbidium* can be neatly repaired with green horticultural twine, so easy and yet seldom practised by orchid growers unless they have been shown. Take a length of twine and tie it to the undamaged centre leaves leaving two ends long enough to finish the job. Twist the string several times and loop it around the next leaf, gradually drawing up each damaged leaf, and repeating the operation until all leaves are held in their original position, finishing with a knot. If the leaves do not hold themselves erect it may require a cane in the compost to act as a support. After some months, the bases of these leaves will have healed and the string can be removed.

The semi-rigid leaves of paphiopedilums can be broken all too easily. This damage, particularly if to a new leaf, is unsightly and can spoil the whole appearance. However, it is not completely unrepairable if attended to at once. Examination of the broken leaf will reveal that it is the centre spine which has cracked and the rest has merely kinked. Provided this is supported in its natural position as soon as possible the break will mend without leaving too much of a scar. If left at this unnatural angle for only a few days a repair job will be much harder to carry out. The simplest method of repairing such damaged leaves is to bend the leaf straight and slide a small elastic band of the right size over the leaf. The band will hold the two sides of the leaf closer together and the break will naturally heal. After a few weeks the band may be removed. Alternatively, transparent sticky tape is just as effective. If the end of the leaf is heavy and there is a strain on the break it would also assist to support the end of the damaged leaf with a cane. This method will correct broken leaves on any orchids with a similar problem.

Not all orchids are tidy and attractive plants in their growth; in particular the tall dendrobiums can be very untidy. In their wild state they grow as epiphytes high in the branches of the trees where their long cane-like pseudobulbs hang down under their own weight. When cultivated in pots they are staked to conform to a standard type of culture and also to prevent them from becoming top-heavy. An unobtrusive bamboo cane can be inserted into the compost at the rear of the plant where there is less danger of damaging young roots and new growths. A length of garden twine should be tied securely to the cane and loops placed around each elongated pseudobulb holding them in a loose but firm tie (right). Other tall-growing orchids such as epidendrums will benefit from staking. Staking will also improve the balance of a top-heavy plant, though a safer solution is to place its plastic pot in a larger clay pot or similar container.

It is not unusual for some orchids to flower whilst they are resting in a dormant state. At this time they require no water whatsoever. Our illustration (far right) shows *Calanthe harrisii* which is completely deciduous and the flowers are produced entirely from the energy stored in the pseudobulb during the previous growing season.

Unusual deformities on leaves and new growths can cause concern. The concertina effect or corrugation of the young leaves on odontoglossums is neither a pest nor a disease. It is usually considered to be the result of a cultural defect normally occurring in intergeneric hybrids within the *Odontoglossum* alliance and can also occur on paphiopedilums and cymbidiums. It is the result of irregular growth when the leaves were enclosed within the young shoot. If at that time the plant suffered a severe check either from dryness or extremes in temperature the growth trapped in its own sheath would be distorted and crippled.

Vertical splits in pseudobulbs occasionally occur, mainly in odontoglossums and cattleyas. These can be almost the length of the pseudobulb, cutting deeply into the surface, and result in the secretion of a sap-like substance. The cause is partly genetic and partly cultural. On the cultural side we can help by ensuring that the plant is kept evenly moist. Luckily, odontoglossums do not require a prolonged resting time. There is always a danger of infection as shown in the right-hand picture on p. 134, and the splits should be dusted with captan or sulphur to aid healing.

All too often the symptoms of ill health are not recognised until it is too late. Our illustration shows a *Cymbidium* which has, over a long period, been totally overwatered and neglected in so many ways that it is almost completely dead. An orchid is a growing, living organism with the will to live, and under the right conditions it will thrive. However, when it has been allowed to deteriorate through either general neglect or mistaken kindness to a state such as this, there is little help that anyone can offer. All orchids have a built-in tolerance and will cope with a maximum and minimum temperature range beyond the usual recommendations. The amount of water that they can exist on before showing signs of over or underwatering is also amazing. Therefore the greatest of extremes have to be endured before an orchid is reduced to the unhappy state we see here. This was a mature plant which had no doubt been well grown before being subjected to ill-treatment.

The signs which are consistent with neglect on this plant are the premature loss of all but one leaf. The pseudobulbs are shrivelled under the bracts, and the new growths, rapidly using the last reserves, have no chance of making up into pseudobulbs before death will finally overtake them. It is obvious that there will be no live roots on the plant.

Before throwing away a neglected and dead plant it is as well to examine the remains, as we can all learn something from our mistakes. After removing the plant remains from the pot, we discover that it has been so overwatered that the compost had changed from a coarse open mixture to a heavy sour consistency. As a result all the roots had died, which was followed by deterioration of the foliage and finally the pseudobulbs. Although the loss of any plant is always sad we can learn from it. Dead plants should never be left lying around as they can cause secondary infections and more trouble. The death of an orchid can seldom be attributed to just one cause, and general neglect will encourage pests and diseases. Red spider mite and scale insects always thrive on sick plants, taking a heavy toll on the plant in its weakened state, and quickening the end. Overwatering, underwatering, low temperatures and a lack of regular repotting are all contributory factors. Insects or worms will inhabit decomposed compost and it is easy to pick on these secondary causes to blame for the plant's death, when what really happened occurred months earlier. After careful examination the plant should then be consigned to the incinerator, and if the pot is to be re-used it must be thoroughly washed. Clay pots which are not so popular now are harder to sterilise. Plastic pots are more hygienic.

The new growth on odontoglossums appears from inside the basal leaf. The new growth will naturally progress, pushing the basal leaf aside. However, the new roots which come from the base of the growth some time later may become impaired by the leaf and unable to extend immediately into the compost. Although not essential, it can often help to remove the small basal leaf to ensure freedom of growth for the shoot and ample room for the new roots. When the new growth is a few inches high and before the new roots have started, this is the right time to remove the basal leaf. By holding the leaf tip using two hands, split the basal leaf down its central vein, separating the two downwards. Be careful not to damage the growth or any young roots that may have already appeared. There are not many orchids where this leaf removal is beneficial; it is mostly confined to odontoglossums and related hybrids, including miltonias. Miltonias can be slow to produce roots if the conditions are not exactly right, and this will encourage the new roots. Cymbidiums also produce new growths inside a basal leaf, but they sit deeper in the compost and there is little need to assist the growth, as they always manage to root and grow without this help.

Orchid leaves will often live for several years, during which time they can be subjected to conditions which can create spots.

Stanhopeas, which are mainly cool-growing orchids, do well in hanging baskets as they produce their flower spikes from underneath. They can present a problem in the winter when hanging high in the roof of the greenhouse. Here, close to the glass, they are most at home, but this position can present certain problems caused by cold. Unless your greenhouse is warm enough or well insulated, they should be placed on the staging at the coldest times. Plants hanging close to the glass can easily become chilled, and although their leaves remain green and healthy certain areas will suffer and as a result become infected with fungus or bacterial spores creating unsightly markings. These markings are not to be confused with *Cymbidium* virus mentioned on p. 138. This disfigurement cannot be cured or removed as once the leaf cells have died they cannot be turned green again. Although the oldest affected leaves may be removed for the appearance of the plant, it would be a mistake to defoliate a plant completely because its leaves had become spotty. Some plants could take years to recover from the sudden and premature loss of their leaves, especially if, like the *Stanhopea*, each pseudobulb carries a single leaf. Apart from removing the occasional leaf, there is no treatment required.

The art of orchid growing is really no different from the art of growing any plant and is based on an understanding of how the plant grows. We can learn this art from the moment we enter the greenhouse. The first impression on opening the door should be of a moist, buoyant atmosphere which smells right and allows you to feel the humidity and temperature and light combining to make a perfect growing environment. We often overlook the sense of touch, and to feel your orchids and know they feel right is just as important as to look at them. This becomes more important with plants indoors where you lack the greenhouse environment; you will learn to feel the difference between a healthy plump leaf and a dehydrated one. Get yourself into the habit of shaking hands with your orchids – this is not as silly as it sounds! Feeling the leaves as you walk around your greenhouse or room will tell you whether they are plump, firm and healthy. Use the flat part of your hand to grasp the leaf firmly; you will immediately notice that it is cool to the touch, as this part of your hand is the most sensitive to temperature. In this way you can decide whether your orchids are receiving too much light on a sunny day which could burn the leaves.

Orchids within the *Odontoglossum* group are liable to get their young flower spikes trapped in the fold of the basal leaf bracts. These bracts are always tight at their base where they hug the sides of the semi-flattened pseudobulb. The flower spikes on this group of orchids come from the base of the pseudobulb and develop within the leaf bract. Although the bract will serve the purpose of protecting the spike when young, it may also trap the tip of the spike and prevent it from growing straight. The flower spike continues to grow from the base pushing the tip forward and jamming it even further into the trap. If not spotted in time the result is either a badly-formed flower spike or the spike snapping under its own pressure. This does not happen often but should always be looked for among the odonto-glossums and allied genera. As soon as you notice a flower spike trapped in this way carefully divide the basal leaf from the tip downwards to release the flower spike. A crooked flower spike which has been released will continue to grow, but will not necessarily straighten out. As the spike develops, a supporting cane will take the strain from the crooked base.

Young flower spikes developing within the bracts can be found by holding a likely plant up to the light. A flower spike will show up as a dark shadow under the bract. This is a good time to release the tip of the bract to ensure the flower spike does not become trapped.

CARE OF FLOWERS

We have discussed the importance of caring for your orchids and how attention to small details in their grooming leads to an overall improvement in their appearance. Removing a blackened leaf tip here and the odd yellow leaf there and not allowing dead material to lie around in the greenhouse all raises the standard of orchid culture culminating in well-grown, beautifully-produced plants. The ultimate of all this grooming is flowering. Few orchids are grown for their foliage alone; most are expected to produce a magnificent display of flowers. Having successfully groomed your plant for a complete growing season with the accumulative effect of good culture over many years, it is an exciting climax to see the plant coming into flower spike. These flower spikes or buds will require their own special attention, depending on the varieties, to ensure that in the weeks that follow they give of their best. Many of the botanical species, especially the small dainty ones, require little or no staking, but larger hybrids such as cymbidiums, which can produce upright spikes of 15–25 blooms, 3–4 ft (90–120 cm) long, need a little more care and attention. Mostly their heavy spikes are not capable of supporting themselves and must have an assisting cane. Smaller flower spikes may require no staking and wherever possible allow the flowers to follow their natural habit. Staking should always be the means by which you bring out the best in your flowers to produce a pleasing effect, and should be kept to a minimum.

In their natural environment growing on trees high above the ground the epiphytic species grow upwards towards the light. Mostly, however, their flower spikes hang outwards or down. Sometimes these are extremely long, producing a wonderful display of blooms. Orchids with pendent flower spikes can be grown in baskets, and indeed stanhopeas can only be grown in baskets as the flower spikes grow from the base of the plant and straight through the bottom. Some pendent flower spikes start horizontally and creep across the surface of the compost before plunging over the rim of the pot. *Cymbidium devonianum* is notorious for its flower spikes plunging straight into the compost before reaching the pot rim. Because of its very thick, fleshy root system it is better grown in a pot than in a basket and therefore care has to be taken to ensure that the flower spike does not disappear. In late summer the newly developing spike can be distinguished from the flatter new growth, and by placing a label underneath the flower spike and over the pot rim you will ensure that it is guided safely across the surface to hang naturally downwards. No attempt should be made to stake *Cymbidium devonianum* or other pendent spikes in an upright position. This will probably result in the spike snapping at some stage. For travelling to shows, you will have no problem if you lay your plant of *Cymbidium devonianum* flat on a sheet of tissue or newspaper with the flexible spikes placed as if upright. The plant is easily rolled up in a paper tube, in which it will safely travel with no harm coming to the flowers.

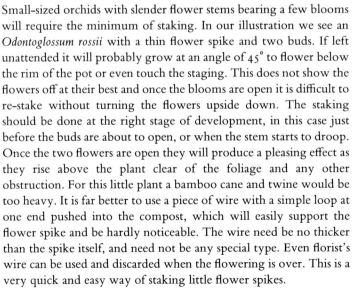

Small-sized orchids with slender flower stems bearing a few blooms will require the minimum of staking. In our illustration we see an *Odontoglossum rossii* with a thin flower spike and two buds. If left unattended it will probably grow at an angle of 45° to flower below the rim of the pot or even touch the staging. This does not show the flowers off at their best and once the blooms are open it is difficult to re-stake without turning the flowers upside down. The staking should be done at the right stage of development, in this case just before the buds are about to open, or when the stem starts to droop. Once the two flowers are open they will produce a pleasing effect as they rise above the plant clear of the foliage and any other obstruction. For this little plant a bamboo cane and twine would be too heavy. It is far better to use a piece of wire with a simple loop at one end pushed into the compost, which will easily support the flower spike and be hardly noticeable. The wire need be no thicker than the spike itself, and need not be any special type. Even florist's wire can be used and discarded when the flowering is over. This is a very quick and easy way of staking little flower spikes.

Of the most popular orchids in cultivation cymbidiums produce the largest and most robust flower spikes. From an early stage they will require sturdy support and some form of training, often before the buds are showing. Whereas some are naturally straight and upward-growing, others are produced at such an angle that they appear to be shooting straight across the staging. It is these latter spikes which are more difficult to train and in the most need of it! Place a light bamboo cane, pointed and of a suitable length, in the position you would like to see the flower spike, which may be upright or at a slight angle to improve the appearance. Always insert the cane at the rear of the plant close to the flower spike and well away from the pot rim so as not to damage the main root system. Tie the spike securely to the cane near the base. It may be necessary to retie several times during the flower spike's development, each time bringing it a little closer to the cane. The loop of string should form a collar through which the spike can grow naturally and especially when ties are placed above the fast growing first flower bud, a daily check should be made that none of the ties have become too tight. Also at this stage do not move the plants more than is necessary so that the light influence does not change.

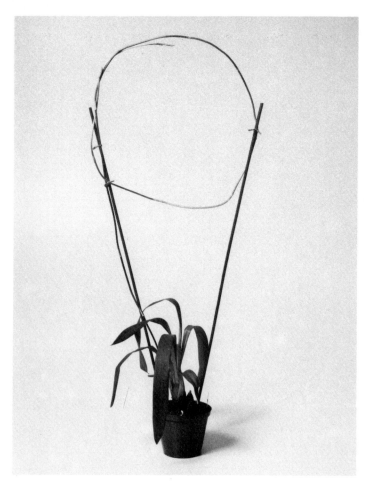

It is the nature of some orchids to produce extremely long flower spikes. This is especially so amongst some *Oncidium* species and their hybrids. *Oncidium macranthum* is quite capable of producing a flower spike of 10 ft (3 m) on a mature plant. This is a daunting thought to a grower with a small greenhouse! However, these extremely long flower spikes are flexible and easily trained. Two light bamboo canes are placed in the pot at opposite sides of the plant forming a V shape. These will enable you to train the flower forming a V shape. These will enable you to train the flower spike up one cane, and as it progresses you can bring it round in a loop, attach it to the other cane and allow it to grow across to form a perfect circle. The end of the spike can continue in a circle for as long as it grows. This can also be done on a horizontal plane forming an upright spiral effect. *Oncidium macranthum* and its hybrids do not produce flowers from the main stem, but from branches which are developed later. Each branch is capable of carrying four, five or even six flowers. These branches will stand out from the hooped spike and be very effective. In the wild, these long spikes hang down from the trees where the species grow, forming a display of cascading blooms. Sensitive to the slightest breeze, they would be continually moving.

Be sure only to hoop the flexible flower spikes. Some are far too rigid and would snap before yielding. You can easily test the spikes to determine their flexibility before training.

This is a safe and attractive staking method for certain orchids, and enables them to be carried to shows without further attention.

The majority of flower spikes will form a natural arch from where the buds start. The supporting cane can stop here, with one tie at the top or just below the second bloom. As the flowers open, the end of the spike will become increasingly heavy, and extra support may have to be given. A cross cane positioned at an angle from the pot to somewhere near the end buds is a good idea when transporting the plant. The end of the spike is secured to prevent it from waving about during transit. This extra supporting cane is ideal for travelling and will ensure its safe arrival, although it should not be necessary at home. If a spike is in danger of breaking or bending under its own weight some extra support will be necessary which is less obtrusive than the extra cane. To achieve this a length of strong wire is inserted into the hollow end of the shorter bamboo cane, and bent carefully to follow the natural arch of the flower spike terminating before the end bud, with an occasional tie. This will be hardly noticed particularly when the flowers are fully opened.

Most *Odontoglossum* type flower spikes will need training from about 6 in (15 cm) high to arrive at the final positioning of the flowers.

During their development, buds will make small changes in their direction as they constantly adjust to the natural position with the dorsal petal at the top of the undeveloped bud. Once the flowers are open they become set and nothing will make them change that position. Therefore you should foresee the angle at which you wish the spike to develop and the habit that is most pleasing. If the flower spike is not staked until after the flowers have opened, the result will be flowers on their sides with lips pointing at an unnatural angle (above). This, of course, will spoil the whole effect. A flower bud has still to open at the top of the spike and may well develop to a new attitude adding still further to the problem. If the plant is staked again the appearance will be even worse. Once the blooms open they quickly set and there is little time in which staking or alteration of the habit can be changed. Careful attention and great expertise is needed if changes are to be carried out at this stage.

One of the few exceptions to open flower staking are the paphiopedilums. Here it is best to allow the stem to grow naturally, particularly with the modern hybrids, which produce large heavy blooms. If the stem is staked firmly in an upright position as it develops, and the flower held tightly before the bloom is set, then it is liable to droop and become set in a less attractive position. Allow the flower to open fully before placing a single tie at the back of the bloom. This will support the flower and show it off to its best advantage. This principle applies to the large modern hybrids. The lighter-flowered, mottled-leaved types need very little staking, and some of the small dainty species will need the bent wire staking previously described. A group of species typified by *Paphiopedilum bellatulum* produce very short stems, some no more than an inch (2.5 cm) long. These may need careful individual staking as soon as the bloom is fully opened; others can be left with no stake.

Where a plant has more than one bloom facing in different directions, it is possible to make them all face the same way. For exhibition this can make a tremendous difference in the placing of a plant. Proceed as described above, for the modern hybrids, tying the opened and set flower to a thin cane no higher than the reverse side of the flower. Place an extra tie reasonably tight lower down on the main stem. It should now be possible to twist the cane and the flower will twist around with it. In this way all flowers can be twisted to face one direction.

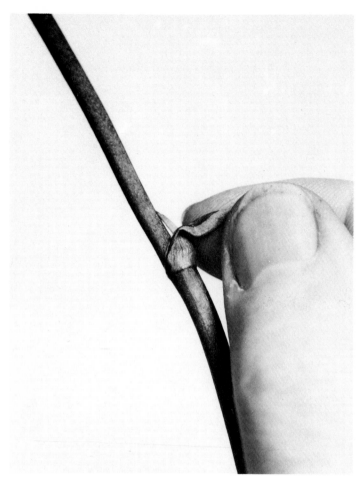

In some *Oncidium* hybrids, mostly those with *Oncidium incurvum* and *sphacelatum* in their background, a defect can occur where the heavy sheathing which protects the embryo branches on the side of the main stem is liable to become hard and prevent the buds on the branch from developing. Where this condition exists it usually follows that the only branches and buds to develop are those at the very end of the spike. Early attention to the eyes further down the stem will encourage extra branches to develop and more blooms. It will be noticed that each embryo branch is covered in a scale-like sheath. By carefully peeling this back the young shoot will be exposed which will immediately grow and form a branch with flowers. Peel the sheath back to reveal the branch, but do not remove it altogether as the base could be harmed if it is torn away from the stem. Sometimes branches which have not been assisted will continue to grow tight to the main stem, and do not pull away at a wide enough angle to hold their flowers clear of the main stem.

Do not attempt to peel back the sheaths until the flower spike has finished growing in its length. Only then will the branches begin to grow. The species *Oncidium incurvum* and some of its hybrids will start its flower spike twelve months prior to flowering. As winter approaches, the spike rests, to continue again in the spring and flowering eventually in late summer. Any peeling of sheaths here need not be done before the summer.

By turning the sheath away from the young shoot at an early stage the side branches quickly develop and the flower buds start to form. These branches may not have had the chance to develop without this assistance. Only hybrids which have been bred from naturally-branching species will benefit from this. Bracts that are peeled back from the lower half of the stem of odontocidiums and wilsonaras may not always develop branches. These will only occur on the top two thirds of the stem. If the flower spike should lose its tip it will produce a side shoot from one of these bracts which will take over the terminal growth of the original spike. This will also happen with phalaenopsis which can produce a side spike from embryo eyes lower on the stem. Only a few orchids behave in this way. Certain warm-growing hybrids which have been bred from *Miltonia spectabilis* have a tendency for the blooms to follow in a sequence. The heavy sheathing of the flower buds forces the blooms in a cluster at the end of the stem. With these hybrids, the removal of the sheathing at a late stage of their development will greatly assist the spread of the blooms on the spike.

Cattleyas and their related hybrids produce flowers from the top of tall, club-shaped pseudobulbs at the base of one or a pair of leaves. From the junction of these leaves with the pseudobulb a large green sheath is most often produced in which the flower buds develop. This sheath bears some resemblance to a large pea pod. The sheath is automatically developed at the same time as the new growth is completed. It forms part of the growing sequence of the pseudobulb and foliage, but does not necessarily mean that the buds are produced at the same time. Many cattleyas complete their growth in the autumn but the flower buds may not appear until the following spring. By holding the plant up to the light, or shining a torch through the sheath, the development of the embryo bud inside can be monitored. At first it will appear as a small swelling in the base of the sheath. Gradually the buds will develop until the sheath splits open and the growing buds emerge and flower. Sometimes the end of the sheath has no natural split, or maybe is so well sealed that the buds find it impossible to force their way out. Deformed buds will attempt to open within the sheath. A careful watch to observe if the buds are becoming trapped is important. If necessary, slightly squeeze the end of the sheath to cause it to pop open like a pea pod, which will assist the clear passage of the buds.

Once the flower bud of a *Cattleya* has successfully emerged from the sheath it will develop rapidly and open its bloom in a few weeks, or in some cases even in a few days. Cattleyas are the fastest flowering orchids from the time the buds are first seen. Most of the early development will have taken place within the sheath. As soon as the flowers are open they will require some attention especially as the modern hybrids can be as large as dinner plates and can hang rather unattractively on their short stems. Each flower, especially on plants that have three or four blooms on a head, will require individual staking. A similar method of staking and tying as recommended for paphiopedilums will serve this purpose. However, a more interesting technique preferred by orchid growers is to use a split bamboo cane placed just behind the bloom. First take a cane of suitable length and split one end with a penknife. Insert the other end into the compost, in an upright position where your bloom will be. The back of the flower is rested in the split, which can then be lowered or twisted to allow the bloom to be held in the most perfect position. Where several blooms are produced on a single stem the flowers will need to be arranged so that they are equally spaced apart. It is a technique which requires practice. If the split is too tight it will bruise the stem, and if it is too loose it will fail to hold the flowers as required. The final result should have all the blooms facing the same way.

INDEX OF PLANTS